Celtic Blessings

BRENDAN O'MALLEY is Chaplain of the University of Wales, Lampeter and Officer for Pastoral Development and Renewal in the Diocese of St David's, Wales. He is of Irish descent, Scottish birth and education, Welsh adoption and is a former Cistercian monk. His interests lie particularly in pilgrimage and in monastic and Celtic spirituality. His previous publications include the award-winning *The Animals of St Gregory* (Paulinus Press, 1981); *A Pilgrim's Manual, St David's* (Paulinus Press, 1985); *A Welsh Pilgrim's Manual* (Gomer Press, 1989); *Celtic Spirituality* (Church in Wales Publications, 1992); *God at Every Gate* (Canterbury Press, 1997) and *Pilgrim Guide to St David's* (Canterbury Press, 1997).

CW00732306

CELTIC BLESSINGS

Making all things sacred

compiled by

BRENDAN O'MALLEY

CANTERBURY
PRESS
Norwich

ACKNOWLEDGEMENTS

Unless otherwise mentioned the scripture verses quoted in this publication are from The Revised English Bible (REB). My warmest thanks are due to Jane Main for drafting the typescript. Every effort has been made to trace the copyright holders of material quoted in this book. Information on any omissions should be sent to the publishers who will make full acknowledgment in any future editions.

BRENDAN O'MALLEY

© in this compilation Brendan O'Malley 1998
First published in 1998 by The Canterbury Press Norwich
(a publishing imprint of Hymns Ancient & Modern Limited
a registered charity)
St Mary's Works, St Mary's Plain,
Norwich, Norfolk, NR3 3BH

British Library Cataloguing in Publication Data

A catalogue record for this book is available
from the British Library

ISBN 1–85311–199–6

*Typeset by David Gregson Associates, Beccles, Suffolk
Printed and bound in Great Britain by
Biddles Ltd, Guildford and King's Lynn*

*To Richard and Gyll Matthews
who blessed me with their daughter,
Rosemary Morwenna.*

Contents

DEEP PEACE
OF THE
RUNNING WAVE TO YOU
DEEP PEACE
OF THE SILENT STARS
DEEP PEACE
OF THE
FLOWING AIR TO YOU

INTRODUCTION

DEEP PEACE
OF THE QUIET EARTH
MAY PEACE
MAY PEACE, MAY PEACE
FILL YOUR SOUL
LET PEACE
LET PEACE, LET PEACE
MAKE YOU
WHOLE

INTRODUCTION

Blessed be the God and Father of our Lord Jesus Christ, who has conferred on us in Christ every spiritual blessing in the heavenly realms. Before the foundation of the world he chose us in Christ to be his people, to be without blemish in his sight, to be full of love; and he predestined us to be adopted as his children through Jesus Christ. This was his will and pleasure in order that the glory of his gracious gift, so graciously conferred on us in his Beloved, might redound to his praise. In Christ our release is secured and our sins forgiven through the shedding of his blood. In the richness of his grace God has lavished on us all wisdom and insight. He has made known to us his secret purpose, in accordance with the plan which he determined, beforehand in Christ, to be put into effect when the time was ripe: namely, that the universe, everything in heaven and on earth, might be brought into a unity in Christ.

The Letter of Paul to the Ephesians 1:1–10

Jesus Christ is the Word made flesh, in him humankind finds the perfect unity or 'blessing', a blessing in which everything human is taken up and given in response to the God who has spoken. In the life of Jesus, the Word of God is made flesh, for we know how God acts through

1

our knowledge of Christ. The blessing that Jesus pronounces is fulfilled in the supreme act of his existence, the Cross. The Cross is no longer a sign of painful death and loss but a sign of victory through the resurrection. The Sign of the Cross is a symbol of the restoration of creation to its primitive condition, full of joy and former goodness. It is *the* symbol of unity.

God has blessed us by providing for us, he has created all things and knows that they are good. He has given us resources and in his Son he has intervened to show us the Way back to him. He has given us many blessings and we in return praise and bless him for his gifts. That is, we thank him, and anything we bless is acknowledged as a gift from him and, as it were, offered back to him through its right use, and in the spirit of the gospel towards the building up of creation to the greater glory of God.

To bless is to call actively for the grace or gift of God himself, who justifies and sanctifies us in an action done in his name. It is to elicit a sure response from God to the cry of his children for love and attention. God's reply calls forth from our hearts an echo to the sacred, inner sound of his word, which is a thanksgiving for all that he has done and for all that we do in his name.

In a real sense all blessings are eucharistic, manifestations of the moment when Christ took bread, blessed it and broke it. It is through the Eucharist or Thanksgiving of the Cross that we offer ourselves as a living sacrifice to God. In the Eucharist, in the communion of the Mystery, we find ourselves and all things filled with the very life of God. The Eucharist itself is *the* great blessing through which all of creation is brought into the oneness of God.

The consecrated bread, or host (from the Latin *hostia* – victim), is the microcosm of the macrocosm; the centre of the hourglass, as it were, through which all things flow and are brought together. It is the ultimate symbol (*symballo* – to throw together, *diaballo* – to throw apart) of the blessing, that is the inner contact which unifies the heavenly and the earthly. All blessings reflect the eucharistic pattern and most blessings show this. We, too, are to be a blessing for others, as St Augustine said: 'to be taken, blessed, broken, distributed that the work of the Incarnation may go forward'.

The purpose and effect of a blessing over any object or activity, person or circumstance is not so much to alter the symbol or inner life of its reality: it is to thank God for the gift of its existence and use, and to offer that use back to him. By blessing any object we thank him for the medium in which we shall use it, and for the way God's goodness is revealed through it. In this sense it is to make the object very special.

Crosses, medals, pilgrim tokens such as the scallop shell, icons, candles and other religious articles have long been used as a means of fostering and expressing our religious devotion to God and the saints. They are an aid to Christian piety and devotion. The use of any religious article is therefore intended as a means of reminding us of God, and of stirring up in us a ready willingness and desire to serve God and our neighbour. It is important to realize that objects which are blessed for any use are not fetishes that work magically by just being had or worn or said. It requires voluntary effort based on faith in order to achieve the purpose for which they were instituted. A blessed article for spiritual use can never be divorced from the faith of the person who uses it.

Many of the blessings in this book may be used by lay people; however the blessing of spiritual articles (such as a cross or a pilgrim medal) and the blessing of water should be reserved for a priest. Blessing by lay people reveals what is already part of the faith of a Christian, that those who are baptized have certain privileges as sharers in the royal priesthood of Christ. Hence lay people may effectively bless and give blessing (cf. Genesis 12:2; Luke 6:28; Romans 12:14; 1 Peter 3:9), but the more a blessing concerns ecclesial and sacramental life, the more is its administration reserved to the ordained ministry.

A blessing combines the divine and the human, radically affirming the dignity of every person as a child of God. When we bless in the name of the Father, the Son and the Holy Spirit, we share the Peace which is at the centre of the triune God. The Peace establishes a fraternity which builds up the Body of Christ.

This book is entitled *Celtic Blessings*, and it includes other blessings for everyday use. To the Christian Celts the whole of life constituted a blessing, and their enjoyment of it is reflected in collections of prayers and blessings, such as

The Carmina Gadelica, by Alexander Carmichael.

There is a great desire in our time for the mystery inherent within all of creation to be connected to daily life. The blessing of all and everything is a good habit which will effect God's presence in the minutiae of our lives. It was the Welshman, St David, who said 'Lords, brethren, and sisters, be joyful, and keep your faith and belief, and perform the little things which you have heard and seen with me' (*Rhygyfarch's Life*). This down-to-earth approach was more of a heaven-to-earth experience. As in the taught experience of the Eastern Orthodox Church, saints were not those who had 'passed on', as it were; their presence is still with us. The angels and saints are as much a part of the Body of Christ as we are, and they live on in our blessing; as, for example, in the Hebridean's word at parting with lover or wife or friend: 'The blessing of God go with you and the blessing of Columba.' To bless another is to pass on our own self, to share with him or her something of the spirit of your love and strength. So it comes about that Iona's saint lives on in that warm farewell, his presence at one's side, and his prayer for safeguard.

These blessings are collected and offered so that we may enjoy, in a fuller way, the 'little things' and use them to the greater glory of God.

How to Use this Book

This book is a handbook for everyday use. A blessing involves healing, peace, consecration of places and space. It may be that holy water may be needed to aid the action of blessing an article, object or person, and so a rite is included. Blessing is both spiritual *and* physical and they need to be in balance, therefore the use of the Sign of the Cross and holy water is to be encouraged. The Contents lists the headings relating to the various main blessings. However, any of the prayers and blessings may be used as the celebrant deems fit. The collection of Celtic Blessings towards the end of the book are ideal for post-eucharistic or prayer-service use.

> The Father, the Son, the Holy Spirit,
> Save you, and shield you, and tend you,
> Till I or mine shall meet you again.
> *Carmina Gadelica*

BLESSING OF WATER

YOU ARE
TO BE
TAKEN
BLESSED
BROKEN
DISTRIBUTED
THAT THE
WORK
OF THE
INCARNATION
MAY GO
FORWARD

BLESSING OF WATER

There is an old saying that the devil hates holy water! It evidently reminds him of holy baptism and the Christian promise to fight against evil. The practising Christian, on the other hand, should love holy water, since by the means of it he or she began the new life in Christ, and became a member of his Mystical Body, the Church.

In addition to its use as a reminder of baptism and remission of sin, holy water is a sacramental, that is, something which conveys a blessing through the intercession of the Church. Thus, when water is blessed, a blessing is invoked upon all who use it and upon all objects on which it may be sprinkled.

Rite for the Blessing of Water

Dear friends,
this water will be used
to remind us of our baptism.
Let us ask God to bless it
and to keep us faithful
to the Spirit he has given us.

God our Father,
your gift of water
brings life and freshness to the earth;
it washes away our sins
and brings us eternal life.

We ask you now
to bless † this water
and to give us your protection on this day
which you have made your own.
Renew the living spring of your life within us
and protect us in spirit and body,
that we may be free from sin
and come into your presence
to receive your gift of salvation.[1]

*The priest/minister sprinkles himself and the
assembled people.*

A small drop of water
To thy forehead, beloved,
Meet for Father, Son and Spirit,
The Triune of power.

A small drop of water
To encompass my beloved,

Meet for Father, Son and Spirit,
The Triune of power.

A small drop of water
To fill thee with each grace,
Meet for Father, Son and Spirit,
The Triune of power.

Carmina Gadelica III, 21.[2]

You are our breath. You are the flight
    of our longing to the depths of heaven.
You are the water which flees from
    the wilderness of our anxiety and fear.
You are the salt which purifies.
You are the piercing wind of our pomposity.
You are the traveller who knocks.
You are the prince who dwells within us.

Waldo Williams

BLESSING OF OIL

GRANT, WE PRAY,
THAT THOSE WHO
WILL USE THIS OIL,
WHICH WE ARE ✢
BLESSING IN YOUR
NAME, MAY BE ✢
DELIVERED FROM
ALL SUFFERING,
✢ ALL INFIRMITY,
AND ALL WILES OF
THE ENEMY

JAMES 5 : 14-15

BLESSING OF OIL

Just as holy water, which is intended for everyday use, is to remind us of the water of baptism, so also blessed oil, a sacramental, is to remind us of the sacrament of anointing. There is a blessing for oil which is 'non-sacramental', i.e. for oil which is blessed for everyday use, and which people may use at home when praying for each other. The use of this oil need not be limited to the sacrament of anointing or to bishop or priest, although its blessing is reserved to the bishop or priest.

Rite of Anointing

Priest: Our help is in the name of the Lord.
All: Who made heaven and earth.

Jesus said, 'I have come that they may have life, and may have it in all its fullness.' (John 10:10)

Reading: James 5:14–15
Is any among you sick? Let him call for the elders of the church, and let them pray over him, anointing him with oil in the name of the Lord; and the prayer of faith will save the sick man, and the Lord will raise him up; and if he has committed sins, he will be forgiven.

Priest: Lord, heed my prayer.
All: And let my cry be heard by you.
Priest: The Lord be with you.
All: And also with you.
Priest: Let us pray.

Lord God almighty, before whom the hosts of angels stand in awe, and whose heavenly service we acknowledge; may it please you to regard favourably and to bless † and hallow † this creature, oil, which by your power has been pressed from the juice of olives. You have ordained it for anointing the sick, so that, when they are made well, they may give thanks to you, the living and true God.

Grant, we pray, that those who will use this oil, which we are blessing in your name, may be delivered from all suffering, all infirmity, and all wiles of the enemy.

13

Let it be a means of averting any kind of adversity from man and woman, made in your image and redeemed by the precious blood of your Son, Christ our Lord. Amen.

Our Father, who art in heaven,
hallowed be thy name;
thy kingdom come;
thy will be done,
on earth as it is in heaven.
Give us this day our daily bread.
And forgive us our trespasses,
as we forgive those who trespass against us.
And lead us not into temptation,
but deliver us from evil.
For thine is the kingdom,
the power, and the glory,
for ever and ever. Amen.

God, sanctifier of this oil, as you give health to those who use and receive (that) with which you anointed kings, priests, and prophets, so may it give strength and health to all that use it.

Hippolytus

To you be glory, to the Father and the Son with the Holy Spirit, in the holy Church, both now and always and to all the ages of ages. Amen.

RITES OF PASSAGE

They do not leave;
they are not gone.
They look
upon us still.
They walk among
the valleys now,
they stride upon
the hill.
Their smile is in the
summer sky,
their grace is in
the breeze.
Their memories
whisper in the grass
their calm is in the
trees.
Their light is in the
winter snow,
their tears are in
the rain.
Their merriment
runs in the brook,
their laughter in
the lane.
Their gentleness
is in the flowers,
they sigh in autumn
leaves.
They do not leave;
they are not gone.
Tis only we who
grieve

RITES OF PASSAGE

For everything its season,
and for every activity under heaven its time;
a time to be born and a time to die,
a time to plant and a time to uproot;
a time to kill and a time to heal ...

Ecclesiastes 3:1–3

Baptism is the sacramental equivalent to natural birth, and the Church, too, is a Mother who gives birth to her children in the font. At baptism she gets new clothes, a candle to light her way, water to help her grow, oil for strength, even companions for the journey. But that is only the beginning of a much longer journey.

A child takes its first few faltering steps. Parents watch excitedly, anxiously, hopefully, hands outstretched to catch her if she falls. And fall she does. But the process is irreversible, other steps follow. Childhood is sign-posted with firsts: first day at school, mother holds her hand as she tearfully and fearfully leaves the cosiness of home and mother's love for the tougher, noisy world of classroom and playground. Church life and teaching launch her into another world, the sacramental and the sacred.

Years pass, each bringing its own firsts as she nervously makes her way through adolescence: first dance, first love, first job, first flat ... rites of passage, pilgrim's progress, steps along a road never to be travelled again. Each step into the unknown, each step in hope. In fact hope is just taking the first step.

The next step is marriage. Paths cross, love blossoms, engagement follows. Each walks up the aisle alone, last steps of a separate existence.

Central to every step or 'sign' in life is the physical and the spiritual. Central to every sacrament is the 'sign' too: for example, water in baptism, a ring in marriage. Ordinary things of this earth are taken and, joined to a word, for example: 'I baptize you ...' or 'I anoint you ...' become means of grace.

This section of blessings is intended to be a complement to the sacramental prayers, rites and blessings of our Mother the Church. They also include rites of blessing for those who, like the woman at the well, are seeking forgiveness, renewal of spirit and a new direction.

Blessing of a Child

There is a mother's heart in the heart of God.
And 'tis his delight to break the bread of love
and truth for his children.

A Hebridean Mother

I send my heart to Thee in thanks for these little
ones: for the strange uprising of happiness that
comes to me as my eye follows them. Sweet is
the music of their wind-borne laughter, yea,
sweeter than all musics. I listen to them, and
am one with the mavis and the dawn and the
flower. And then I wonder what Thy thought is
of them – Thy children. Yet I need not wonder.
For I look upward and lo! Thou art leaning out
over the window of Heaven, and Thou art smil-
ing.

Hebridean

I bless thee, darling one, in the name of the Holy
Three, the Father, the Son, and the Sacred
Spirit. Thine may it be to drink deeply from
God's cup of joy. May the sun be bright upon
whatever road thou farest. May the night bring
thee quiet. And when thou art come to the
Father's palace may His door be open and the
welcome warm!

Blessing of a Hebridean Grandmother

Thou who art high,
Send down from the sky
The Angels Three,
That while I sleep,
My babe they keep
From harm and fear.
So shall I feel
That Thou art near
When they are nigh,
And myself sleep
Without a care,
Without a sigh.

Hebridean

The Dedication of a Child

V.   Our help is in the name of the Lord.
R.   Who has made heaven and earth.

V.   Our God shows mercy
R.   The Lord is the keeper of his little ones.

V.   O Lord hear my prayer
R.   And let my cry come unto you.

V.   The Lord be with you
R.   And also with you.

Let us pray:
Lord Jesus Christ, Son of the living God, you were begotten before time began yet willed to become an infant in time, showing love for the age of innocence; you also lovingly embraced and blessed the little children, who were presented to you. Aid this infant (child or children) with blessings of sweetness and let not wickedness alter its (their) understanding. Grant also to this child (children) such growth in age, wisdom and grace as will render him/her/them always pleasing to you, who live and reign with God the Father in the unity of the Holy Spirit, God world without end. Amen.

The child/infant may be blessed with a symbol of blessing such as holy water.

May the peace and blessing of God Almighty, Father, Son † and Holy Spirit, descend upon you and remain for ever. Amen.

and/or

May the love of the Father enfold us,
the wisdom of the Son enlighten us,
the fire of the Spirit inflame us;
and may the blessing of the triune God rest
    upon us,
and abide with us, now and evermore.
Amen.

Scottish

A Mother's Consecration

Be the great God between thy two shoulders,
To protect them in thy going and thy coming,
Be the Son of Mary Virgin near thine heart,
And be the perfect Spirit upon thee pouring –
Oh, the perfect Spirit upon thee pouring!

Hebridean

Thanksgiving for
a Safe Delivery

Merciful Lord, we thank you for the deliverance
of your servant N from the pain and anxiety of
childbirth. Grant, we pray you, that through
your help she may live faithfully according to
your will, and praise you not only with her lips
but in her life; through Jesus Christ our Lord.
Amen.

Welsh

For the Parents

Almighty God, giver of life and love, grant that
each of these your servants may be to the other
a companion in joy, a comfort in sorrow, and a
strength in need; and so join their wills together
in your will, and their spirits in your Spirit,
that they may live together in peace and love
all the days of their life; through Jesus Christ
our Lord. Amen.

Welsh

The grace of our Lord Jesus Christ,
and the love of God,
and the fellowship of the Holy Spirit,
be with us all evermore. Amen.

Parents' Prayer for their Children

Lord God! You have called us to the holy state of matrimony and have been pleased to make us parents. We recommend to you our dear children. We entrust them to your fatherly care. May they be a source of consolation, not only to us, but chiefly to you who are their Creator. Be watchful, O Lord; help and defend them.

Grant us the grace to guide them in the way of your commandments. This we will do by our own example. Make us conscious of our grave obligation to you and bless our efforts to serve you. We humbly ask this blessing from the depths of our hearts, for ourselves and for our children whom you have been pleased to give us.

We dedicate them to you, O Lord. Keep them as the apple of your eye and protect them under the shadow of your wings. Make us worthy to come, at last, to heaven, together with them giving thanks to you, our Father and our Mother, for the loving care you have had of our family, and praising you together through endless ages. Amen.

Bless ourselves and our children,
Bless every one who shall come from our loins,
Bless him whose name we bear,
Bless, O God, her from whose womb we came.

Every holiness, blessing and power,
Be yielded to us every time and every hour,
In name of the Holy Threefold above,
Father, Son, and Spirit everlasting.

Gaelic

Children's Prayer for their Parents

Dear Lord! Fill our parents with your choicest blessings; enrich their souls with your holy grace. Grant that they may faithfully and constantly guard the vows of love they made on their wedding day. Fill them with the spirit of peace, patience and wisdom; inspire them to impart it to their children. May they ever walk in the way of truth and may their children be their joy on earth and their crown of glory in heaven.

Finally, Lord God, grant that both our father and mother may attain to old age and enjoy continuous health in mind and body. May they give abundant thanks to you who have bestowed upon them the great gift of parenthood. Through Jesus Christ our Lord. Amen.

A Mother's Parting Blessing

The blessing of God be to thee,
The blessing of Christ be to thee,
The blessing of Spirit be to thee,
And to thy children,
To thee and to thy children.

The peace of God be to thee,
The peace of Christ be to thee,
The peace of Spirit be to thee,
During all thy life,
All the days of thy life.

The keeping of God upon thee in every pass,
The shielding of Christ upon thee in every
    path,
The bathing of Spirit upon thee in every
    stream,
In every land and sea thou goest.

The keeping of the everlasting Father be thine
Upon his own illumined altar;
The keeping of the everlasting Father be thine
Upon his own illumined altar.

Carmina Gadelica III, 247

Hearken, fair son of my love, to me
Torn with love 'twixt keeping thee
And bidding thy heart
From my heart depart
To win the dream I cannot see.
Whate'er thy morrow
Of sun or sorrow,

27

May God comrade at thy side
His arm thy bield*,
His love thy shield,
'Gainst chance's barb or change's tide.

Gaelic: Source unknown

* *bield*: a shelter or habitation.

A Family Prayer

Father, we bring to you
the needs of all our families.
We call you Father
because we are all your children.
Let your fatherly love
strengthen our family
and all families
in peace and harmony,
in love and faithfulness,
in care and considerateness
for each other,
in faith and patience
in our difficulties,
in hope and forgiveness,
in prayer and cheerfulness,
through our Risen Lord
in the unity of the Holy Spirit,
now and forever.
Amen.

Source Unknown

A Service for the Renewal of Marriage Vows

Sentence:
God is love, and those who live in love live in God; and God lives in them. (1 John 4:16)

Introduction:
Joy is the companion of love, as N and N have celebrated their love in marriage, this element of joy is an important part of this whole ceremony of the blessing of their marrige. Like love, joy is something that is shared. We all have a share in the joy of N and N who will acknowledge today the total gift of themselves to one another.

I invite you all to let their joy show through your participation with them in this celebration of that love.

Prayer:
Father, you have made the bond of marriage a holy mystery, a symbol of Christ's love for his people. Hear our prayers for N and N as with faith in you and each other they renew the pledge of their love today. May their lives always bear witness to the reality of that love. Through Jesus Christ our Lord. Amen.

Reading: The Love of Christ (Romans 8:31b–35, 37–39)
With God on our side who can be against us? Since God did not spare his own Son, but gave him up to benefit us all, we may be certain, after such a gift, that he will not refuse anything

he can give. Could anyone accuse those that God has chosen? When God acquits, could anyone condemn? Could Christ Jesus? No! He not only died for us – he rose from the dead, and there at God's right hand he stands and pleads for us.

Nothing therefore can come between us and the love of Christ, even if we are troubled and worried, or being persecuted, or lacking food or clothes, or being threatened or even attacked. These are the trials through which we triumph, by the power of him who loved us. For I am certain of this: neither death nor life, no angel, no prince, nothing that exists, nothing still to come, not any power, or height or depth, not any created thing, can ever come between us and the love of God made visible in Christ Jesus our Lord.

(Alternative readings: 1 Corinthians 13:1–7, or The Beatitudes, Matthew 5:1–12a.)

Homily

A hymn may be sung.

RENEWAL OF MARRIAGE VOWS

Priest: We have come together in the presence of God because you wish to ask God's blessing on your marriage. The Scriptures teach that marriage is a gift of God in creation and a means of his grace, a holy mystery in which man and woman became one flesh. In marriage husband and wife belong to one another, and they live a life together in the community. It is a way of life that all should honour, and it must not be undertaken carelessly, lightly, or selfishly, but reverently, responsibly, and after serious thought.

This is the way of life, created and hallowed by God, that you have begun. You have given consent to one another and you have joined hands and exchanged solemn vows, in token of which you have both given and received a ring. Therefore, on this day we pray that, strengthened and guided by God, you may fulfil his purpose for the whole of your earthly life together.

Take the rings for blessing
Most Holy God, bless these rings (*or* ring), grant that they who wear them may be faithful to each other and continue bound together in love to their lives' end. Through Jesus Christ our Lord. Amen.

The couple silently place the rings on each other's fingers.

N and N, you have come together in this church so that Christ may seal and strengthen your love – Christ abundantly blesses your love. He has already consecrated you in marriage and now he enriches and strengthens you in the renewal of your vows so that you may continue to perform the duties of marriage in mutual and lasting fidelity. And so, in the presence of the community of Christ, before me, its minister, and with these friends and family as witnesses, I ask you to renew your intentions to live in lifelong fidelity to each other and to God in whose image you have been made.

Priest to the man: N, do you acknowledge N as your wife?
Man answers: I do.

Priest: Will you live with her in obedience to God's will and purpose? Will you love her, honour her and care for her, in sickness and in health? Will you be faithful to her, and her alone, as long as you both live?
Man answers: I will.

Priest to the woman: N, do you acknowledge N as your husband?
Woman answers: I do.

Priest: Will you live with him in obedience to God's will and purpose? Will you love him, honour him and care for him, in sickness and in health? Will you be faithful to him, and him alone, as long as you both live?
Woman answers: I will.

The couple together: We believe that we are meant to be for each other a sign of Christ's love. We believe that we are called to bring one another to God. We believe that we are called to give ourselves in service to God and humankind. We believe that we are meant to help our children look beyond us and give themselves in service to God and humankind. Believing these things, we offer ourselves together, as man and wife, to God, so that our love may become his love, through Christ our Lord. Amen.

Hymn

Intercessions:

Almighty and Everlasting God, strengthen these your servants, N and N with your grace, that they may keep the promises they have made in your presence.
Lord in your mercy,
R. Hear our prayer.

Let your peace be in their home and your blessing upon it.
Lord in your mercy,
R. Hear our prayer.

We pray that the peace of Christ may abide in our world, our nation, our families and our hearts.
Lord in your mercy,
R. Hear our prayer.

Make your love known through N and N and their home, that your holy Name may be glorified.
Lord in your mercy,
R. Hear our prayer.

We pray that married couples everywhere may understand it is love alone which unites them.
Lord in your mercy,
R. Hear our prayer.

All say together: Our Father ...

(A hymn may be sung here.)

The Blessing:

Let us ask God for his continued blessing upon you both.
(All pray silently for a short while.)

Holy Father, creator of the universe, maker of man and woman in your own likeness, source of blessing for married life, we humbly pray to you for N and N who today seek your blessing through the renewal of their marriage vows. May your fullest blessing come upon them so that they may together rejoice in your gifts of married love.

God the eternal Father keep you in love with each other so that the peace of Christ may stay with you and be always in your home. Amen.

May your family bless you, your friends console you, and all people live in peace with you. Amen.

May you always bear witness to the love of God in this world so that the afflicted and the needy will find in you generous friends, and welcome you into the joy of heaven. Amen.

And may Almighty God bless you, the Father, the Son, and the Holy Spirit. Amen.

Prayers and Blessing for Those whose Relationship has Ended

V. Lord, have mercy upon us.
R. Christ, have mercy upon us.
V. Lord, have mercy upon us.

Our Father ...

Prayers:
Father of all mercies and giver of all grace, we commit ourselves to you and ask for your guidance and help in our new life apart. Guide us in the days ahead and help us in our perplexities and self doubt. We offer and present to you, Lord, ourselves, our souls and bodies, our thoughts and our deeds, our desires and our prayers. We ask you to forgive anything in us which has been amiss, to take us as we are, and to make us what you would have us be, through Jesus Christ our Lord. Amen.

Take away, O Lord, from our hearts all suspiciousness, indignation, anger and contention, and whatever is calculated to wound charity. We ask this for your Son's sake, Jesus Christ our Lord. Amen.

Lord, I offer up to you those whom I have in any way grieved, hurt or scandalized, by word or deed, knowingly or unknowingly; that you may equally forgive us all our sins, and all our offences against each other, through Jesus Christ our Lord. Amen.

Almighty and everlasting God, you are always more ready to hear than we are to pray, and to give more than either we desire or deserve; pour down upon us the abundance of your mercy, forgiving us those things of which our conscience is afraid and giving us those good things which we are not worthy to ask but through the merits and mediation of Jesus Christ, your Son, our Lord. Amen.

Grant, O Lord, that your Holy Spirit may lead us in the way of wisdom and understanding, that we may obey your will and seek to serve you till our lives' end.

May Almighty God pour upon us the riches of his grace, sanctify and bless us, so that in the days ahead we may please him in body and soul. Amen.

The grace of our Lord Jesus Christ, and the love of God, and the fellowship of the Holy Spirit be with us evermore. Amen.

Welsh (adapted from The Book of Common Prayer, Church in Wales)

Blessing of the Elderly

V.   Our help is in the name of the Lord.
R.   Who made heaven and earth.

A reading from the prophet Zechariah (8:4–5):

I shall come back to Zion and dwell in Jerusalem. Jerusalem will be called the City of Faithfulness, and the mountain of the Lord of Hosts will be called the Holy Mountain. These are the words of the Lord of Hosts: once again old men and women will sit in the streets of Jerusalem, each leaning on a stick because of great age; and the streets of the city will be full of boys and girls at play.

Psalm: 71:1–3, 17–18.

Response: Do not forsake me, Lord my God.

1. In you, Lord, I have found refuge;
   let me never be put to shame.
   By your saving power rescue and deliver me;
   hear me and save me!
Response

2. Be to me a rock of refuge
   to which at all times I may come;
   you have decreed my deliverance,
   for you are my rock and stronghold.
Response

3. You have taught me from my childhood, God,
   and all my life I have proclaimed your marvellous works.
   Now that I am old and my hair is grey,

do not forsake me, God, until I have extolled
   your strength
to generations yet to come.

Response

Let us pray:
May the right hand of the Lord keep us even
   in old age,
the grace of Christ continually defend us from
   the enemy.
O Lord, direct our heart in the way of peace;
through Jesus Christ our Lord. Amen.

*From the Book of Cerne, the prayer book of Bishop Aedelwald,
eighth century*

Service of Blessing for
a Still-Born Child

Thus says the Lord: 'In a time of favour I have
answered you, on a day of salvation I have
helped you.' . . . But Zion said, 'The Lord has for-
saken me, my Lord has forgotten me.' 'Can a
woman forget her nursing child, or show no
compassion for the child of her womb? Even
these may forget, yet I will not forget you. See,
I have inscribed you on the palms of my hands.'
(Isaiah 49:8, 14–16 NRSV)

Psalm: 84: 3–7, 11.

Response: My soul is longing for the courts of
the Lord.

1. The sparrow finds herself a home
   and the swallow a nest for her brood;
   she lays her young by your altars,
   Lord of hosts, my king and my God.
Response

2. They are happy, who dwell in your house,
   for ever singing your praise.
   They are happy, whose strength is in you,
   in whose hearts are the roads to Sion.
Response

3. As they go through the Bitter Valley
   they make it a place of springs.
   They walk with ever growing strength,
   they will see the God of gods in Sion.
Response

4. For the Lord God is a rampart, a shield;
   he will give us his favour and glory.

The Lord will not refuse any good
to those who walk without blame.
Response

While Jesus was by the lakeside, there came a
synagogue president named Jairus; and when
he saw him, he threw himself down at his feet
and pleaded with him. 'My little daughter is at
death's door,' he said. 'I beg you to come and
lay your hands on her so that her life may be
saved.' So Jesus went with him. (Mark 5:21–22)

Homily

Prayers

God our Creator,
from whom all life comes,
comfort this family,
grieving for the loss of their hoped-for child.
Help them to find assurance
that with you nothing is wasted or incomplete,
and uphold them with your love,
through Jesus Christ our Saviour.
Amen.

Lord Jesus,
full of tenderness for little ones
and for the humble,
you notice and are concerned
about a single sparrow that falls to the
    ground.
We know that you have seen
the fall of our little sister/brother N.
We are confident that you will receive her/him
with joy into your kingdom.

We make this prayer through Christ our Lord.
Amen.

Take N into your heart, O Lord,
that he/she may be closer to us.
And may the blessing of almighty God,
the Father, and the Son † and the Holy Spirit,
come upon N and upon us
and remain with us all for evermore.
Amen.

I bless thee for the secret voice which tells me
I am dear to thee.
I worship thee because
I know the voice for thine.

Hebridean

I am going home with thee,
Thou child of my love,
To the dear Son of blessings,
To the Father of grace.

I am going home with thee,
Thou child of my love,
To thine eternal bed,
To thy perpetual sleep.

Gaelic

The angel said, 'I shall complete the journey
with him. Do not be afraid.' (Tobit 5:21)

Blessing of the Dead

Beannacht De le hanama na marbh
(The blessing of God on the souls of the dead.)
Ta siad imithe ar shli na firinne
(They are gone on the way of truth.)
Irish

Let the Great Shepherd lead and by winding
    ways,
not without green pastures and still waters,
we shall climb insensibly and reach the tops of
    the everlasting hill,
where the winds are cool and the sight is
    glorious.
Scottish

Father of all, we pray to thee for those we love,
but now no longer see.
Grant them thy peace;
let light perpetual shine upon them;
and in thy loving wisdom and almighty power
work in them the good purpose of thy perfect
    will; through Jesus Christ our Lord. Amen.
Welsh

Thou goest home this night to thy home of
    winter,
to thy home of autumn, of spring, and of
    summer;
Thou goest home this night to thy perpetual
    home,
To thine eternal bed, to thine eternal slumber.
Scottish Gaelic

Lord, now lettest thou thy servant depart in peace.

Truly I say to you, today you will be with me in Paradise.

Into thy hands we commend his/her spirit: for thou hast redeemed him/her, thou God of truth.

Go forth, Christian soul, out of this world,
In the Name of God, the Almighty Father, who
   created you;
In the name of Jesus Christ, his Son, who
   redeemed you;
In the name of the Holy Spirit, who sanctifies
   you.
May the holy angels help and defend you;
May your Redeemer look upon you in pardon
   and mercy;
May your rest be in peace and your dwelling-
   place in the paradise of God.

Welsh Book of Common Prayer 11

V. May the souls of the faithful departed,
   through the mercy of God, rest in peace.
R. And rise in glory.

Give them rest with the devout and the just,
in the place of the pasture of rest and of
   refreshment,
of waters in the paradise of delight,
whence grief and pain and sighing have fled
   away.

From an Early Christian Prayer

Death

> Thou great God of salvation,
> Pour thy grace upon my soul
> As the sun of the heights
> Pours its love on my body.
>
> I must needs die,
> Nor know I where or when;
> If I die without thy grace
> I am lost everlastingly.
>
> Death of oil and of repentance,
> Death of joy and of peace;
> Death of grace and of forgiveness,
> Death of Heaven and life with Christ.
>
> *Carmina Gadelica III, 373*

Death with Unction

Death with unction and with penitence,
Death with joy and with forgiveness,
Death without horror or repulsion,
Death without fear or shrinking.

Dying the death of the saints,
The Healer of my soul by my side,
The death of peace and tranquillity,
And grant thou me a good day of burial.

The seven angels of the holy Spirit
And two attendant angels
Be shielding me, and be this night the night
Till brightness and summer-tide shall come!

Carmina Gadelica III, 377

They do not leave, they are not gone.
   They look upon us still.
They walk among the valleys now,
   they stride upon the hill.
Their smile is in the summer sky,
   their grace is in the breeze.
Their memories whisper in the grass,
   their calm is in the trees.
Their light is in the winter snow,
   their tears are in the rain.
Their merriment runs in the brook,
   their laughter in the lane.
Their gentleness is in the flowers,
   they sigh in autumn leaves.
They do not leave, they are not gone.
Tis only we that grieve.

Source unknown, possibly Scottish

God has not taken them from us.
He has hidden them in his heart
that they may be closer to ours.

VISIT,
WE BESEECH
THEE, O LORD,
THIS HOME,
AND DRIVE AWAY
FROM IT ALL
SNARES OF THE
ENEMY; LET THY
HOLY ANGELS
DWELL HEREIN TO
PRESERVE US IN
PEACE AND LET
THY BLESSING
ALWAYS BE UPON
US. THROUGH
CHRIST
OUR LORD
AMEN

HEARTH
AND HOME

HEARTH AND HOME

To bless a home is to open the door of the heart of the family to the presence of the indwelling God. It is to create a 'sacred space' where people are made more consciously aware of the activity of the Holy Spirit. To use the words of blessing is to commit a sacred act for words, too, can be sacred, and they become sacramental when what is said has been 'sacramentalized' in the name of Christ.

As the individual is cleansed through prayer and sacramental activity, so is a place designated as a home, a dwelling for God's love in the domestic family. The prayers and blessings in this section may be used for personal prayer and meditation.

Blessing of a Home

The King is knocking. If thou would'st have thy share of heaven on earth, lift the latch and let in the King.

Hebridean

On entering:

> Peace of God be unto you,
> Peace of Christ be unto you,
> Peace of Spirit be unto you,
> Peace be to your children too,
> To your children and to you.

Trad. Gaelic

V.   The Lord is here.
R.   God's Spirit is with us.

> God bless the house,
> From site to stay,
> From beam to wall,
> From end to end,
> From ridge to basement,
> From balk to roof-tree,
> From found to summit,
> Found and summit.

Carmina Gadelica I, 105

> God, bless the world and all that is therein,
> God, bless my spouse and my children,
> God, bless the eye that is in my head,
> And bless, O God, the handling of my hand;
> What time I rise in the morning early,

What time I lie down late in bed,
Bless my rising in the morning early,
And my lying down later in bed.

God, protect the house, and the household,
God, consecrate the children of the
    motherhood,
God, encompass the flocks and the young;
Be Thou after them and tending them,
What time the flocks ascend hill and wold,
What time I lie down to sleep,
What time the flocks ascend hill and wold,
What time I lie down in peace to sleep.

Carmina Gadelica I, 103

The person blessing the house may perform a *caim*, or encompassing, a form of blessing which is a form of safeguarding common in the highlands of Scotland and in Ireland since early times. The encompassing of any of the three persons of the Trinity, or of the Blessed Virgin Mary, or of any of the apostles, or of any of the saints may be invoked, according to the faith of the suppliant. In making the *caim* the suppliant stretches out the right hand with the forefinger extended, and turns round sunwise as if on a pivot, describing a circle with the tip of the forefinger while invoking the desired protection. The circle encloses the suppliant and accompanies him as he walks onward, safeguarding from all evil without or within.

The compassing of God and his right hand
Be upon my form and upon my frame;
The compassing of the High King and the
    grace of the Trinity
Be upon me abiding ever eternally,
Be upon me abiding ever eternally.

May the compassing of the Three shield me in
    my means,
The compassing of the Three shield me this
    day,
The compassing of the Three shield me this
    night
From hate, from harm, from act, from ill,
From hate, from harm, from act, from ill.

Carmina Gadelica III, 103

*The Rite for the Blessing of Holy Water may be
appropriate here, and the blessed water used to
sprinkle both the outside and inside of the house
whilst repeating the following prayer:*

The compassing of God be on thee,
The compassing of the God of life.

The compassing of Christ be on thee,
The compassing of the Christ of love.

The compassing of Spirit be on thee,
The compassing of the Spirit of Grace.

The compassing of the Three be on thee,
The compassing of the Three preserve thee,
The compassing of the Three preserve thee.

Carmina Gadelica III, 105

Visit, we beseech Thee, O Lord, this home,
and drive away from it all snares of the
    Enemy;
let Thy holy Angels dwell herein
to preserve us in peace
and let Thy blessing always be upon us.
Through Christ, our Lord. Amen

Blessing of an Entrance Hall

Everyone who asks receives, those who seek find, and to those who knock, the door will be opened. (Luke 11:10)

I sleep, but my heart is awake. Listen! My beloved is knocking. (Song of Solomon 5:2)

'Behold I stand at the door and knock,' says the Lord. 'If you hear my voice and open the door, I will come in and eat with you and you with me.' (Revelation 3:20)

A symbol of blessing may be used.

Creator Spirit of God, come to those who belong to you, and fill them with your grace. Enlighten our minds, warm our hearts, and with your power strengthen our weakness.

She whom I love I greet with my heart's blood,
But all my senses fail in the wild storm of
　love.

Come, Holy Spirit of Wisdom and Truth,
enter our hearts and enkindle in them the
　Fire of your love.

Spirit of hearth and home,
joyous and Divine Guest, full of love and
　laughter,
make this dwelling a place for creativity and
　inspiration,
peace and renewal,
a home where N and N find happiness
　everlasting,
Amen.

May God give blessing
To the house that is here;

May Jesus give blessing
To the house that is here;

May Spirit give blessing
To the house that is here;

May Three give blessing
To the house that is here.

Gaelic

There is a door to which thou hast the key
Sole keeper thou.
There is a latch no hand can lift save thine.
Not crowned brow,
Nor warrior, thinker, poet-famed in time,
But only thou.
O heart make haste and bid him to thy hearth.

Nay, urge him in.
So shall thy night be gone with all thy dearth,
So shalt thou win
Joy such as lovers know when love is told,
Peace that enricheth more than miser's gold.

Hebridean

I wait with love's expectancy.
Lord Jesus, trouble not to knock at my door.
My door is always on the latch.
Come in, dear guest, and be my host
and tell me all thy mind.

Ancient Gaelic

Blessing of a Living Room

V.   Lord, God of all creation,
R.   You are ever welcome in this house.

Let us listen to the Word of God.

Are you chosen to preside at a feast? Do not put
on airs; mix with the others as one of them.
Look after them and only then sit down yourself; discharge your duties before you take your
place. Let the enjoyment of others be your pleasure, and you will win a garland for good man-
ners. (Ecclesiasticus 32:1–2)

O Clement one,
O Imparter of true wisdom,
O Ruler of speech,
O Spirit of wisdom,
O Spirit of understanding,
O Spirit of counsel,
O Spirit of strength,
O Spirit of knowledge,
O Spirit of affection,
O Spirit of love,
O Spirit of grace,
O Holy Spirit that rules all things, visible and
    invisible,
Have mercy upon us.
O Almighty God, the heavenly Father, and
O only begotten Son.
Have mercy upon us,
Have mercy upon us, O Father, O Son,
O Holy Spirit.
Have mercy upon us, O only God,

O God of heaven, have mercy upon us.
Have mercy upon us, O God,
from whom and through whom
is the rule of all created things for thee, O
   God.
To thee be glory and honour for ever and
   ever,
Amen.

Adapted from an Early Irish Litany

A symbol of blessing may be used.

Father, Son and Sacred Spirit,
The One and the Three,
Bless † preserve and protect from all evil
all those who shall sit or talk or work together
   here.
May they share your care and understanding.
Lord of the gentle heart
May they be gentle too.

V.   Let us bless the Lord.
R.   Thanks be to God.

May the Lord direct our hearts into God's love
   and Christ's perseverance.
Amen.

Blessing of a Kitchen

Mary's Son, my Friend, cometh
to bless my kitchen ...
My kitchen,
The kitchen of the white God,
A kitchen which my king hath blessed,
A kitchen that hath butter.

Book of Lismore

V. The eyes of all wait upon you O God.
R. And you give them their food in due season.

A symbol of blessing may be used.

Creator, Sustainer and Life-giver,
food shared between mother and child is your
   first gift,
is the first taste we know of love.
May the food we prepare,
the work of love done in this room,
be a sign that you dwell for ever with us
in the everyday things of your world.

You shall eat in plenty and be satisfied,
and praise the name of the Lord your God,
who has dealt so wondrously with you.

May Christ our constant guest
make our humblest meal a welcome offering.

Blessing of a Dining Area

I saw a stranger today.
I put food for him in the eating-place
And drink in the drinking-place
And music in the listening-place.
In the Holy Name of the Trinity
He blessed myself and my family.
And the lark said in her warble
Often, often, often
Goes Christ in the stranger's guise
O, oft and oft and oft,
Goes Christ in the stranger's guise.

Celtic Rune of Hospitality

V. The living God gave you from heaven rain
    and fruitful seasons satisfying your hearts
    with food and gladness.
R. God brings forth food from the earth and
    wine to gladden the heart.

A symbol of blessing may be used.

Blessed are you, Sovereign of the universe
for gifts from your bounty which we receive.
May our hearts be thankful;
may we always have room for a guest.

Make us grateful for all your mercies
and mindful of the needs of others.

Blessing of a Study/Place of Prayer and Meditation

> With Jesus to find restfulness
> In the blest habitation of peace,
> In the paradise of gentleness,
> In the fairy-bower of release
> Mercy arrayed.
>
> *Traditional Gaelic*

Help us, O God, in the search for true wisdom, and show us the path that leads to understanding.

A symbol of blessing may be used.

> God, the source of all wisdom,
> May this be a place of reflection and
>   awareness,
> of knowledge and understanding.
> Show yourself for us,
> lest we go about in ignorance;
> reveal yourself to us,
> for in you we know the incarnate Word.
> Amen.

Before Sacred Reading or Study:

God I offer you every prayer, thought, word and work for all the intentions of thy divine Heart. Amen.

Lord, may my whole being be directed to your service and praise. Amen.

Set a watch, O Lord, upon my mind and my soul, that I do not incline to evil thoughts or distractions during this time of sacred reading and study. Amen.

Blessing of a Bathroom

The one who is unclean must wash his clothes and bathe in water, and at sunset he will be clean. (Numbers 19:19)

I will sprinkle you with clean water, and you will be cleansed. (Ezekiel 36:25)

Prayer:
Blessed are you Lord God of the rain, the streams, the waters and the lakes. Be a living wellspring within us for healing of body, mind and spirit. When we wash here may it be a symbol of our baptism, the refreshment of our inner life and health. Through Jesus Christ our Lord. Amen.

Blessing of a Child's Room

Gentle Jesus, meek and mild,
Look upon a little child.
Pity my simplicity,
Suffer me to come to thee.

They brought children for Jesus to touch, and the disciples scolded them for it. But when Jesus saw this he was indignant, and said to them, 'Let the children come to me; do not try to stop them, for the kingdom of God belongs to such as these. I tell you, whoever does not accept the kingdom of God like a child will never enter it.' And he put his arms around them, laid his hands upon them, and blessed them. (Matthew 19:13–15)

Prayer:
Heavenly Father,
We thank you for calling us to know you,
for leading us to trust you,
and for binding our life with yours.

A symbol of blessing may be used.

We ask you to bless this room and surround
   N with your love;
protect N from all that may harm him/her.
Fill him/her with your Holy Spirit;
and enable him/her to grow and walk in the
   way of Christ.
We pray that N's angel
whom God has appointed to be her/his
   guardian,

enlighten, protect, direct and lead him/her in
   the right path
both now and for evermore. Amen.

Prayers:
   Four angels round my bed,
   Two at the foot and two at the head.
   Matthew, Mark, Luke and John,
   Bless the bed that I lie on.

   Jesus, tender Shepherd, hear me,
   Bless Thy little lamb tonight.
   Through the darkness be Thou near me,
   Keep me safe till morning light.

Bed Blessing

I am lying down tonight,
With Mary mild and with her Son,
With the Mother of my King,
Who is shielding me from harm.

I will not lie down with evil,
Nor shall evil lie down with me,
But I will lie down with God,
And God will lie down with me.

God and Mary and Michael kindly
And the cross of the nine angels fair,
Be shielding me as Three and as One,
From the brow of my face to the edge of my
    soles.

I beseech Peter, I beseech Paul,
I beseech Mary, I beseech the Son,
I beseech the trustful Apostles twelve
To preserve me from hurt and harm;
from dying tonight,
From dying tonight!

God! O Mary of Glory!
O Jesu! Son of the Virgin fragrant,
Sain* Ye us from the pains everlasting,
And from the fire fierce and murky,
From the pains everlasting,
And from the fire fierce and murky!

Carmina Gadelica I, 89

---

* To cross oneself as a sign of consecration or protection.

I lay me down with thee, O Jesus
And mayest thou be about my bed,
The oil of Christ be upon my soul,
The Apostles' Creed be above my head.
Father who wrought me
O Son who bought me
O Spirit who sought me
Let me be thine.

Esther de Waal

Sleep Blessing

Be thy right hand, O God, under my head,
Be thy light, O Spirit, over me shining.
And be the cross of the nine angels over me
down,
From the crown of my head to the soles of my
feet,
From the crown of my head to the soles of my
feet.

O Jesu without offence, crucified cruelly,
Under ban of the wicked thou wert scourged,
The many evils done of me in the body!
That I cannot this night enumerate,
That I cannot this night enumerate.

O thou King of the blood of truth,
Cast me not from thy covenant,
Exact not from me for my transgressions,
Nor omit me in thy numbering.
Nor omit me in thy numbering.

Be the cross of Mary and of Michael over me
in peace,
Be my soul dwelling in truth, be my heart
free of guile,
Be my soul in peace with thee, Brightness of
the mountains.
Valiant Michael, meet thou my soul.
Morn and eve, day and night. May it be so.

Carmina Gadelica I, 67

Blessing of a Guest Room

Be thou my vision, O Lord of my heart;
Naught be all else to me, save that thou art.
Thou my best thought, by day or by night,
Waking or sleeping, thy presence my light.

Trad. Irish

When I was hungry, you gave me food;
when thirsty, you gave me drink;
when I was a stranger, you took me into your
home. (Matthew 25:35)

A symbol of blessing may be used.

Blessed are you Lord God, giver of all good gifts
which we receive with thankful hearts. May
we always receive and welcome you in our
guests.
Open the door of our hearts that we may continue to serve you all the days of our lives,
Through Jesus Christ, our Lord. Amen.

> Both man and woman,
> Both wife and children;
>
> Both young and old,
> Both maiden and youth;
>
> Plenty of food,
> Plenty of drink,
> Plenty of beds,
> Plenty of ale;

Much of riches,
Much of mirth,
Many of people,
Much of long life
Be ever there.

Gaelic

Blessing of a Garden

Sentence:

I will give thanks to the King of grace
For the growing crops of the ground,
He will give food to ourselves and to the
    flocks
According as he disposeth us.

Carmina Gadelica I, 249

Reading:

The fountain in my garden is a
spring of running water
flowing down from Lebanon.
Awake, north wind, and come, south wind,
Blow upon my garden to spread its spices
    abroad,
that my beloved may come to his garden
and enjoy the choice fruit.
(Song of Songs 4:15–16)

Prayer:

Almighty God, Creator:
The morning is yours, rising into fullness,
The summer is yours, dipping into autumn,
Eternity is yours, dipping into time.
The vibrant grasses, the scent of flowers,
The lichen on the rocks, the tang of
    seaweed,
All are yours.
Gladly we live in the garden of your
    creating.

George Macleod

Blessing:

There is no plant in the ground
But is full of his virtue,
There is no form in the strand
But is full of his blessing.

Carmina Gadelica I, 39

And may his blessing be upon this garden that it
may bear fruit in plenty
And be a reflection of the abundant love of our
Lord and Saviour,
Jesus Christ, our Lord. Amen.

TABLE BLESSINGS

MAY THE
BLESSING
OF THE FIVE
LOAVES AND
THE TWO FISHES
WHICH GOD SHARED
OUT AMONG THE
FIVE THOUSAND
BE OURS.
MAY THE
KING WHO DID
THE SHARING BLESS
OUR SHARING
AND OUR
PARTAKING

OLD IRISH

Scottish Graces

Lord, who blessed the loaves and fishes,
Look doon upon these twa bit dishes,
And though the taties be but sma',
Lord, make 'em plenty for us a';
But if our stomachs they do fill,
'Twill be another miracle.

Traditional

The Selkirk Grace

Some hae meat, and canna eat
And some wad eat that want it;
But we hae meat and we can eat,
And sae the Lord be thankit.

Robert Burns, 1759–96

We are God's guests and 'tis he who keeps the
generous table.

A Lewis man

Gaelic Grace Before Food

Be with me, O God, at breaking of bread,
Be with me, O God, at the close of my meal,
Let no whit adown my body
That may hurt my sorrowing soul.
no whit adown my body
That may hurt my sorrowing soul.

Carmina Gadelica III, 315

Beannachadh Bithidh

I liom, a Dhe, aig bristeadh arain,
Bi liom, a Dhe, ri crich mo loin;
Na leig-sa sur a sios mo chalainn
A ni dubhail dha m'anam broin.
Sur a sios mo chalainn
Ni dubhail dha m'anam broin.

Thanks After Food

Thanks be to thee, O God,
Praise be to thee, O God,
Reverence be to thee, O God,
For all thou hast given me.

As thou hast given life corporeal
To earn me my worldly food,
So grant me life eternal
To show forth thy glory.

Grant me grace thoughout my life,
Grant me life at the hour of my death;
Be with me, O God, in casting off my breath,
God, be with me in the deep currents.

O! in the parting of the breath,
O! be with my soul in the deep currents.
God, be with my soul in sounding the fords,
In crossing the deep floods.

Carmina Gadelica III, 317

Irish Graces

Altu roimh Beile, Grace before Meals

> *Beirmid buiochas do Dhia as ucht an bhia*
> *seo ataimid ag dul a chaitheamh*
> *tre Chriost ar atiarna. Amen.*

> We give thanks to God for this food
> which we are about to eat,
> through Christ, Our Lord. Amen.

Altu tar eis Beile, Grace after Meals

> *Glacamid buiochas do Dhia as ucht an bhia,*
> *seo ataimid tar eis a chaitheamh*
> *tre Chriost ar atiarna. Amen.*

> We give thanks to God for this food
> which we have eaten,
> through Christ our Lord. Amen.

Dr Seamus O'Cathain

May the blessing of the five loaves and the two
    fishes
which God shared out among the five
    thousand be ours.
May the king who did the sharing
bless our sharing and our partaking.

Old Irish

Welsh Graces

Diolchwn i Ti am holl roddion dy ragluniaeth,
yn enw ein Harglwydd Iesu Grist. Amen.

We thank thee for all the gifts of thy
  providence,
in the name of our Lord, Jesus Christ. Amen.

Dr Eirwyn Morgan

Bendithia dy roddion hyn,
a sancteiddia ni yn ein mwynhad ohonynt,
a maddau ein beiau,
yn Iesu Grist ein Harglwydd. Amen.

Bless these gifts,
and sanctify us as we enjoy them,
and forgive us our sins,
through Jesus Christ our Lord. Amen.

Revd Tudur Jones

Dad, yn deulu dedwydd - y deuwn,
A diolch o'r newydd,
Caus o'th law y daw bob dydd
Ein lluniaeth a'n llawenydd.

Father, a contented family – we come,
With renewed thankfulness,
Because from thy hand there comes each day,
Our sustenance and our happiness.

W. D. Williams

Roddwr pob rhoddiad daionus a phob rhodd
 berffaith,
bendithia dy bobl, yma ac ymhob mau,
wrth dderbyn, wrth roi ac wrth rannu.
Trwy'r Croeshoeliedig. Amen.

Giver of every good and perfect gift,
bless thy people, here and everywhere,
in their receiving, their giving and their
 sharing.
Through the Crucified. Amen.

Revd Pennar Davies

Am iechyd da a bwyd bob pryd
Moliannwn di O Dduw.

For good health and every meal
We praise thee O God.

Rt Revd B. N. Y. Vaughan

HEALTH AND HEALING

MAY THE
HEALING STREAM
OF THE
HOLY SPIRIT
FLOW THROUGH
YOUR BODY,
MIND AND SPIRIT,
MAKING YOU
WHOLE. IN THE
NAME OF OUR LORD
JESUS CHRIST.
AMEN

BLAISE GILLESPIE

HEALTH AND HEALING

Christ invites us to take up our cross daily. By following Jesus we develop a different outlook on physical illness and the need for inner spiritual healing. Our Lord invites us to share in his ministry to the sick.

> 'So they set out and proclaimed the need for repentance, they drove out many demons, and anointed many sick people with oil and cured them.' (Mark 6:12–13)

The risen Lord renews this mission ('In my name ... the sick on whom they lay their hands will recover') and continues his work through those who invoke him.

The ministry of prayer, anointing, laying on of the hands and blessing of the sick enable those who are troubled in mind as well as body to build up interior peace. It conveys a healing of the spirit which can, under the will of God, further the restoration of health of mind and body.

At the actual laying on of hands the practitioner needs to be aware that he or she is simply a channel through which the Holy Spirit is working, and the recipient should, if possible, be seeking to accept this work of our Lord.

What if the patient does not recover?

People have got into the way of thinking that if somebody dies, the doctors have failed. But healing is not the same as curing. It is about wholeness of life and you can work for that until the moment you die. A lot of work involves getting people to come to terms with the fact that death is one of the most natural parts of life.

Angelique, a sister who cares for the terminally ill, gave this advice: 'There is a wonder of happiness attached to the adventure or journey of death. Many, many patients are only at ease when they have the privacy to take the step.' There is a time when loved ones need to give them space – allowing them the dignity to die in peace.

We are inclined to feel that we are somehow responsible for stopping people dying. The impulse to rescue is very strong. It is O.K. for people to die – relationships do not have to be for ever. The person who is dying is not always the victim and we are not always the strong one – they have had to confront many issues in their process of living with the advent of their death. They therefore have attained much wisdom. We need to challenge our own assumptions about anyone who has a terminal illness.

The ultimate healing lies through and beyond death.

Blessing of the Sick

Know the love of Christ for you and in you.
He does far more than we can ask or imagine
by the Power of the Holy Spirit in us.
Be filled through all your being
with all the fullness of God.

Hear what the Lord is teaching us through his apostle, Peter.

Praised be the God and Father of our Lord Jesus Christ! In his great mercy by the resurrection of Jesus Christ from the dead, he gave us new birth into a living hope, the hope of an inheritance, reserved in heaven for you, which nothing can destroy or spoil or wither. Because you put your faith in God, you are under the protection of his power until the salvation now in readiness is revealed at the end of time.

This is cause for great joy, even though for a little while you may have had to suffer trials of many kinds. Even gold passes through the assayer's fire, and much more precious than perishable gold is faith which stands the test. These trials come so that your faith may prove itself worthy of all praise, glory, and honour when Jesus Christ is revealed.

You have not seen him, yet you love him; and trusting in him now without seeing him, you are filled with a glorious joy too great for words, while you are reaping the harvest of your faith, that is, salvation for your souls. (1 Peter 1:3–9)

Psalm: 139:13–16, 23–24.

Response: Lord you have examined me and you
know me.

1. You it was who fashioned my inward parts;
You knitted me together in my mother's
womb.
I praise you, for you fill me with awe;
wonderful you are, and wonderful your works.
Response

2. You know me through and through:
my body was no mystery to you,
when I was formed in secret,
woven in the depths of the earth.
Your eyes foresaw my deeds,
and they are all recorded in your book;
my life was fashioned
before it had come into being.
Response

3. Examine me, God, and know my mind;
test me and understand my anxious thoughts.
Watch lest I follow any path that grieves you;
lead me in the everlasting way.
Response

Let us pray:
Lord Jesus Christ, our Redeemer, by the grace
of your Holy Spirit cure the weakness of your
servant, N. Heal his/her sickness and expel all
afflictions of mind and body; mercifully restore
N to full health and enable him/her to resume
his/her former duties, for you are Lord for ever
and ever. Amen.

May the Lord bless you;
may he turn his face toward you,
have mercy on you and convert you
back to the way of the Lord, and
give you peace and health ...
and the blessing of the Sacred Three,
the Father, Son and Holy Spirit
be upon you both now and forever more. Amen.

Book of Mulling. Irish, seventh century

*Hands are laid on the head of the person seeking
healing and the following prayers may be said.*

Through the laying on of these hands and
through our prayer, receive the gift of the healing Spirit of God. May the Holy Spirit, the
giver of all life and healing flow through you
and take away anything that is harming or dis-
turbing you. May he give you his peace and joy
and be with you at every change and turn of
your way. We ask this in the name of Jesus
Christ our Lord. Amen.

Prayer:

God of all grace, my body satisfy;
Christ of the Passion, satisfy my soul;
Spirit of wisdom, grant light to me to lie,
And restore to me repose, making me whole.

Trad. Gaelic

PRAYERS FOR THE USE OF ANOINTED OIL

As with this holy oil you are outwardly anointed, so may our heavenly Father grant that

you be inwardly anointed with the Holy Spirit.
Amen.

The priest/minister, dipping his/her thumb in the
holy oil, anoints the person seeking healing on the
forehead with the sign of the Cross, saying:

N, I anoint you with oil † in the name of our
Lord Jesus Christ.
May our heavenly Father make you whole in
body and mind,
and grant you the inward anointing of his
Holy Spirit,
The Spirit of strength and joy and peace.
Amen.

The almighty Lord, who is a strong tower to all
who put their trust in him, be now and evermore
your defence, and make you believe and trust
that the only name under heaven given for
health and salvation is the name of our Lord
Jesus Christ. Amen.

Prayers for Healing

May the healing stream of
the Holy Spirit
flow through your body,
mind and spirit,
making you whole.
In the name of Our Lord Jesus Christ,
Amen.

Gillespie

May God, my dear, be the healing one;
I set my hand upon thee this day
In the name of Father,
In name of Son,
In name of Spirit of power, I pray,
Three Persons who compass thee alway.

Trad. Gaelic

Thou my soul's Healer,
Keep me at even,
Keep me at morning,
Keep me at noon,
On rough course faring,
Help and safeguard
My means this night.
I am tired, astray, and stumbling,
Shield thou me from snare and sin.

Carmina Gadelica III, 85

Loving Father, I am going into hospital but I shall not be alone, for you will be going with me and you will be beside me all the time. I shall be surrounded by your love and nothing whatsoever will ever be able to separate me from that love. You will be present in the situation from the moment I leave home and so there will be nothing at all to fear.

I know that I am very precious in your sight and that you want only the best for me. I am going into hospital so that the doctors can put right the things that are wrong, but it is you who gave them their special skills. They will help me all they can but it is your healing love which is the greatest force of all and which will restore me to health.

Loving Father, give me a tranquil mind and the calm assurance of your loving presence. Even now I know that you are touching me with your healing hands and that all will be well. Amen.

LORDS, BROTHERS
AND SISTERS, BE
happy AND
keep your FAITH
AND your
BELIEF

WORK
AND
COMMUNITY

AND DO
THE LITTLE THINGS
THAT YOU HAVE⁙
HEARD AND
SEEN ME DO

SAINT DAVID

WORK AND COMMUNITY

The contemplative notion of the Cistercian monk consists of offering up every prayer, work and suffering for all the intentions of the Divine Heart in Christ. The dedication of every action, and of every second to God enables, with time, the permanent concentration of the will towards the building up of God's Kingdom, and brings a full reward: peace of the soul and profound happiness.

'To do the little things' as both St David and Pascal instruct us, 'with as much care as if they were great things' is to find the deepest joy and blessing in him who was the carpenter of Nazareth.

When we speak of work *and* suffering we acknowledge that Jesus Christ's greatest work was done as he hung helpless, nailed and bound on the Cross. We can always use suffering for good, for ourselves and others, if we will co-operate with him. He bids us offer our difficulties in work as well as our pain and disability in union with our Lord's offering of himself on the Cross.

It needs to be remembered that life and its blessings are gifts from God. A sacramental blessing of any object, whether it be vehicle, boat or building, sanctifies the different uses to which that object will be dedicated. It sets it apart for a deeper enjoyment of God's creation.

Blessing of Work

The maker of all things,
The Lord God worship we:
Heaven white with angel's wings,
Earth and the white-waved sea.

Early Irish (translated by Robin Flower)

Lords, brothers and sisters,
be happy and keep you faith
and your belief,
and do the little things
that you have heard
and seen me do.

St David

To do the little things with as much care as if
 they were great things,
because of the majesty of Jesus Christ who
 dwells within us ...
... and to do the great things as if they were
 small and easy,
because of his all-powerfulness.

Pascal: Mystery of Jesus

'And he that sent me is with me, and he hath not
left me alone; for I do always the things that
please him.' (John 8:29)

Prayer:

Lord, hear the prayer of all those who seek to do your work in unity and love. By doing the work you have entrusted to us may we sustain our life on earth and build up your Kingdom in faith. We ask this through Christ our Lord, Amen.

May God the Father watch over you.
R.   Amen.

May God the Son save you from all harm.
R.   Amen.

May God the Holy Spirit prosper the work of your hands.
R.   Amen.

And may the blessing of Almighty God,
the Father, the Son and the Holy Spirit
come down upon you and remain with you
for ever and ever. Amen.

Blessing of Achievement

V.   Our help is in the name of the Lord,
R.   Who has made heaven and earth.

Priest: Let us listen to the word of the Lord as
he speaks to us through the Epistle to
the Hebrews.

With this great cloud of witnesses around us,
therefore, we too must throw off every encumbrance and the sin that all too readily restricts
us, and run with resolution the race which lies
ahead of us, our eyes fixed on Jesus, the pioneer
and perfecter of faith. For the sake of the joy
that lay ahead of him, he endured the cross,
ignoring its disgrace, and has taken his seat at
the right hand of the throne of God.

Think of him who submitted to such opposition from sinners: that will help you not to lose
heart and grow faint. (Hebrews 12:1–3)

Psalm: 1:1–3.

Response: The Lord watches over the way of the
righteous.

1. Happy is the one
who does not take the counsel of
the wicked for a guide,
or follow the path that sinners tread,
or take his seat in the company of scoffers.
Response

2. His delight is in the law of the Lord;
it is his meditation day and night.

He is like a tree
planted beside the water channels;
it yields its fruit in season
and its foliage never fades.
So he too prospers in all he does.
Response

Let us pray:
O Lord we give thanks for all those who co-operate with your grace and through obeying your
holy will complete and perfect all that you
would have them do. We give special thanks
for the gifts shown forth in N and for all that
he/she/they have done to glorify your name.

May the Lord bless you, watch over you,
preserve your going out and your coming in.
May he give you his peace . . .
and the blessing . . .
Book of Mulling, seventh-century Irish

Blessing of a Vehicle

V.   The Lord be with you.
R.   And also with you.

Priest: Let us listen to the Lord as he speaks to us through his Apostle, Paul.

You, my friends, were called to be free; only beware of turning your freedom into licence for your unspiritual nature. Instead, serve one another in love; for the whole law is summed up in a single commandment: 'Love your neighbour as yourself.' But if you go fighting one another, tooth and nail, all you can expect is mutual destruction.

What I mean is this: be guided by the Spirit and you will not gratify the desires of your unspiritual nature. That nature sets its desires against the Spirit, while the Spirit fights against it. They are in conflict with one another so that you cannot do what you want.

Those who belong to Christ Jesus have crucified the old nature with its passions and desires. If the Spirit is the source of our life, let the Spirit also direct its course. (Galatians 5:13–18, 24–25)

Psalm: 121

Response: The Lord will guard you as you come and go.

1. If I lift up my eyes to the hills,
   Where shall I find help?

My help comes only from the Lord,
maker of heaven and earth.
Response

2. He will not let your foot stumble;
   He who guards you will not sleep.
   The guardian of Israel
   never slumbers, never sleeps.
Response

3. The Lord will guard you against all harm;
   He will guard your life.
   The Lord will guard you as you come and go,
   now and for evermore.
Response

Let us pray:
We praise you, Lord God, for you are Ruler of
the Creation which you have made through
your Son; and through him you nurture it with
your loving care.

Grant your blessing † upon this N and bless †
those who use it. We pray that they may not
abuse, harm or destroy your creation, or use
this vehicle to disturb or hurt other people.
May they use it for your honour and glory, for
the benefit and service of others.

Father, listen to our prayer, for we offer it
through Christ our Lord. Amen.[3]

Blessing of a Boat

Helmsman:	Blest be the boat.
Crew:	God the Father bless her.
Helmsman:	Blest be the boat.
Crew:	God the Son bless her.
Helmsman:	Blest be the boat.
Crew:	God the Spirit bless her.
All:	God the Father,
	God the Son,
	God the Spirit,
	Bless the boat.
Helmsman:	What can befall you
	And God the Father with you?
Crew:	No harm can befall us.
Helmsman:	What harm can befall you
	And God the Son with you?
Crew:	No harm can befall us.
Helmsman:	What harm can befall you
	And God the Spirit with you?
Crew:	No harm can befall us.
All:	God the Father,
	God the Son,
	God the Spirit,
	With us eternally.
Helmsman:	What can cause you anxiety
	And the God of the elements
	over you?
Crew:	No anxiety can be ours.

Helmsman:	What can cause you anxiety
	And the King of the elements be
	over you?
Crew:	No anxiety can be ours.
Helmsman:	What can cause you anxiety
	And the Spirit of the elements
	be over you?
Crew:	No anxiety can be ours.
All:	The God of the elements,
	The King of the elements,
	The Spirit of the elements,
	Close over us, ever eternally.

Carmina Gadelica I, 333

IN THE CABIN

> Dear God, be good to me;
> The sea is so wide,
> And my boat is so small.
>
> *Breton Fisherman's Prayer*

V. Lord of the seas, you are ever welcome in this boat.

R. May we hear you in your Word and within our hearts.

Be compassionate as your Father is compassionate. Do not judge, and you will not be judged; do not condemn, and you will not be condemned; pardon and you will be pardoned; give and gifts will be given you. Good measure, pressed and shaken down and running over, will be poured into your lap; for whatever meas-

ure you deal out to others will be dealt to you in
turn. (Luke 6:36–38)

O how good and pleasant it is, when God's people live together in unity. (Psalm 133:1)

A symbol of blessing may be used, saying

The One and the Three, God in Trinity,
you have made us to need each other,
and to grow best with companions;
bless those who shall sit or talk or work here.
May they share your care and understanding.

IN THE SLEEPING QUARTERS

> Guide us waking, O God, and guard us
>   sleeping,
> that awake we may watch with Christ,
> and asleep we may rest in your peace.

V.   I lie down in peace and take my rest.
R.   For it is in God alone that I dwell unafraid.

A symbol of blessing may be used, saying

God of the night,
may this be a holy and blessed place for N (and
   N) and all who may sleep here.
Here may they know you loving presence,
find rest for their fatigue,
and peace for their anxiety.
May your holy angels guard them,
and your continual blessing strengthen them.

Father! O Son! O Spirit Holy!
Be thou, Three-One, with us day and night,
And on the back of the wave as on the
    mountain side
Our Mother shall be with us with her arm
    under our head.
And on the back of the wave as on the
    mountain side
Our Mother shall be with us with her arm
    under our head.

Barra Fishermen

AT THE GALLEY

You shall eat in plenty and be satisfied,
and praise the name of the Lord your God,
who has dealt so wondrously with you.

V.   The eyes of all wait upon you O God,
R.   and you give them their food in due season.

A symbol of blessing may be used, saying

God, Creator and Sustainer of all,
bless the hands that work in this galley,
nourish us with all goodness
and give us grateful hearts for the food we eat.
May the work of love done here
be a sign that you dwell for ever with us in the
    little things of your world.
May Christ our constant guest
make our humblest meal a welcome offering.

Blessing of Crops

I will go out to sow the seed,
In name of Him who gave it growth.

Carmina Gadelica I, 243

V. Our help is in the name of the Lord.
R. Who made heaven and earth.

Let us listen to the Word of God:

In the beginning God created the heavens and the earth. God said, 'Let the earth produce growing things; let there be on earth plants that bear seed, and trees bearing fruit, each with its own kind of seed;' and God saw that it was good. (Genesis 1:1, 11–12)

Psalm: 104: 1–2, 14–15, 24, 27–28.
Response: The earth is full of your riches, Lord.

1. Bless the Lord, my soul.
   Lord my God, how great you are.
   Clothed in majesty and splendour
   and enfolded in a robe of light.
Response

2. You make grass grow for the cattle
   and plants for the use of mortals,
   producing grain from the earth,
   food to sustain their strength,
   wine to gladden the hearts of the people,
   and oil to make their faces shine.
Response

3. Countless are the things you have made, Lord;

by your wisdom you have made them all;
the earth is full of your creatures.
Response

4. All of them look to you in hope
to give them their food when it is due.
What you give them they gather up;
when you open your hand,
they eat their full of good things.
Response

Let us pray:
Blessed are you, Lord God,
Creator of the universe.
You are giver and sustainer of life,
bringing forth the fruits of the earth
to feed and nourish your people.
We cultivate the land and sow the seed,
but you alone, Lord, can give the growth.
Let your blessing lie upon this land,
bringing gentle rains and ripening sun
for a joyful harvest.
Give us the grace to use your gifts well,
that the poor may be fed,
and the hungry filled with good things.
Then and always shall we give you glory,
Father of all,
through your Son, Christ Jesus our Lord.
Amen.[4]

Blessing of Produce

Each meal beneath my roof,
They will all be mixed together,
In name of God the Son,
Who gave them growth.

Milk, and eggs, and butter,
The good produce of our own flock,
There shall be no dearth in our land,
Nor in our dwelling.

In name of Michael of my love,
Who bequeathed to us the power,
With the blessing of the Lamb,
And of his mother.

Humble us at thy footstool,
Be thine own sanctuary around us,
Ward from us spectre, sprite, oppression,
And preserve us.

Consecrate the produce of our land,
Bestow prosperity and peace,
In name of the Father the King,
And of three beloved apostles.

Dandelion, smooth garlic,
Foxglove, woad, and butterwort,
The three carle-doddies,
And marigold.

Carmina Gadelica I, 213

Blessing of New Buildings

V.   Our help is in the name of the Lord.
R.   Who has made heaven and earth.

V.   The Lord be with you.
R.   And also with you.

A priest may bless water, saying:

Lord,
May this water † blessed in your name,
be a sign of your protection
for those who live and work here,
for this new building
and for all things in it.
Protect this place from all harm,
and give all who dwell here your peace
and remain with them now and always.
We ask this blessing through Christ our Lord.
Amen.

The priest sprinkles all the people present with the blessed water to remind them of their baptism. The priest then sprinkles the building as a sign of dedication and blessing.

Blessing of a School

V.   Peace be to this school.
R.   And to all who dwell here.

V.   Our help is in the name of the Lord.
R.   Who has made heaven and earth.

Read John 14:12–21, 23.

Let us pray:
Lord Jesus Christ, who commanded your apostles that whichever house they entered they should pronounce upon it the blessing of peace, sanctify by our ministry this house destined for the education of youth; pour out upon it the abundance of your blessing and peace; may salvation come to them as it came to the house of Zachaeus at your entrance into it: command your angels to guard it and to drive from it all the power of the enemy; fill with the spirit of knowledge, of wisdom and good counsel those who teach therein; sustain with heavenly grace those who are taught therein, that they may grasp with their minds and keep in their hearts and put into practice all the saving truths that are taught them. May all who dwell therein be found pleasing to you in every virtuous work, so as to merit a reception into an everlasting dwelling in heaven hereafter. Through you, O Jesus Christ, Saviour of the world, who live and reign, God, for ever and ever. Amen.

A symbol of blessing may be used.

Blessing of any Object

V.   Our help is in the name of the Lord.
R.   Who made heaven and earth.
Priest: Let us listen to the Word of God:

When in times past God spoke to our forefathers, he spoke in many and varied ways
through the prophets. But in this the final age
he has spoken to us in his Son, whom he has appointed heir of all things; and through him he
created the universe. He is the radiance of
God's glory, the stamp of God's very being, and
he sustains the universe by his word of power.
When he had brought about purification from
sins, he took his seat at the right hand of God's
Majesty on high, raised as far above the angels
as the title he has inherited is superior to theirs.
(Hebrews 1:1–5)

Psalm: 145: 2–9.
Response: I shall extol you my God and King,
and bless your name for ever and ever.

1. Every day I shall bless you
   and praise your name for ever and ever.
   Great is the Lord and most worthy of praise;
   his greatness is beyond all searching out.
Response

2. One generation will commend your works to
      the next,
   and set forth your mighty deeds.

People will speak of the glorious splendour
   of your majesty;
I shall meditate on your wonderful deeds.
Response

3. The Lord is gracious and compassionate,
   long suffering and ever faithful.
   The Lord is good to all;
   his compassion rests upon all his creatures.
Response

Priest: Let us pray to our Father in heaven,
         who has given us this (these) N for our
         use.

Pause for silent prayer

Blessed are you, Lord God, King of the
   universe.
You have made all things for your glory.
Bless † this (these) N,
and grant that we may use it (them)
in your service and for the good of all your
   people.[5]

Do thou, O God, bless unto me
Each thing mine eye doth see;
Do thou, O God, bless unto me
Each sound that comes to me;
Do thou, O God, bless unto me
Each savour that I smell;
Do thou, O God, bless unto me
Each taste in mouth doth dwell;
Each sound that goes unto my song,
Each ray that guides my way,
Each thing that I pursue along,

Each lure that tempts to stray,
The Zeal that seeks my living soul,
The Three that seek my heart and whole,
The Zeal that seeks my living soul,
The Three that seek my heart and whole.

Source unknown (Early Scottish)

Father, we praise you through Christ our Lord.
Amen.

LIKE GRACE DRIPPING OFF
THE TREES
YOUR LOVE POURS ON US
BLESSING AND
WETTING US

JOURNEY BLESSINGS

IT SOAKS US
WITH JOY
AND SPREADS THROUGH
THE BLOOD
OF FELT PASSION

WE LAUD AND GIVE
THANKS
FOR THE DESIRE
AND LONGING TO PRAISE

FORGIVE OUR FALLING AND
CONTINUE TO BE
OUR BELOVED
COMPANION ON THE WAY

BLAISE GILLESPIE

JOURNEY BLESSINGS

St Augustine once said, 'The soul finds rest no-where until it rests in God.' The pilgrimage is an expression of this feeling and is in its essence nothing but a search after God in different places and through different acts. The difference between a tourist and a pilgrim is that a pilgrim seeks an experience of God.

Pilgrimage seems to respond to a profound need of the human being to go beyond the limits of ordinary experience into the mysterious realm of the beyond. The journey has many stages along its way, physical and mystical moments serving as thresholds into new stages of life.

The *experience* of the journey or pilgrimage is essential and the blessing given is not only to protect the traveller, but to dispose them towards an encounter with the Beloved Companion on the Way.

May God shield us by each sheer drop,
May Christ keep us on each rock-path,
May the Spirit fill us on each bare slope,
as we cross hill and plain,
Who live and reign
One God for ever. Amen.

Trad. Gaelic

Jesus, my companion be
On the road I take today,
Through the moor or o'er the sea,
Thou, for me, be guide and stay.
Jesus, my sweet lover! Place
In the heart of all I greet
Love like thine that is a grace

To homing men or roving feet.
Up the hill-way, down the glen,
Past the forest edged with broom,
Where the shadows hide the ben,
Where the rivers deepen gloom,
Radiant, I, thy lovesman go
Free from fear and sain from foe.

Hebridean

Saviour and Friend, how wonderful art thou!
My companion upon the changeful way. The
comforter of its weariness. My guide to the Eternal Town. The welcome at its gate.

Scottish, seventeenth century

Cwm Rhondda

Guide me, O thou great Redeemer,
pilgrim through this barren land;

I am weak, but thou art mighty;
hold me with thy powerful hand:
bread of heaven,
feed me now and evermore.

Open now the crystal fountain
whence the healing stream doth flow;
let the fiery cloudy pillar
lead me all my journey through:
strong deliverer,
be thou still my strength and shield.

When I tread the verge of Jordan,
bid my anxious fears subside;
death of death, and hell's destruction,
land me safe on Canaan's side:
songs and praises
I will ever give to thee.

William Williams, eighteenth-century Welsh

PETITION

Be thou a smooth way before me,
Be thou a guiding star above me,
Be thou a keen eye behind me,
This day, this night, for ever.

I am weary, and I forlorn,
Lead thou me to the land of the angels;
Methinks it were time I went for a space
To the court of Christ, to the peace of heaven;

If only thou, O God of life,
Be at peace with me, be my support,
Be to me as a star, be to me as a helm,
From my lying down in peace to my rising anew.

Carmina Gadelica III, 171

May the blessing of light
be on you, light without and light within.
May the blessed sunlight
shine upon you and warm your heart till it
   glows
like a great peat fire, so that the stranger may
come and warm himself at it, as well as the
   friend.
And may the light shine out of the eyes of you,
like a candle set in the windows of a house,
bidding the wanderer to come in out of the
   storm.
And may the blessing of the rain
be on you – the soft sweet rain.
May it fall upon your spirit so that all the
   little flowers may spring up,
and shed their sweetness on the air.
And may the blessing of the great rains be on
   you,
that they beat upon your spirit and wash it
   fair and clean,
and leave there many a shining pool where the
   blue
of heaven shines, and sometimes a star.
And may the blessing of the earth
be on you – the great round earth;
may you ever have a kindly greeting
for people you pass as you are going along the
   roads.
And now may the Lord
bless you, and bless you kindly.

Old Irish Blessing

Prayer:

Heavenly Father, protector of all who trust in you, you led your people in safety through the desert and brought them to a land of plenty. Guide me as I begin my journey today. Fill me with your spirit of love. Preserve me from all harm and bring me safely to my destination. I ask this through Christ our Lord. Amen.

Welsh

Or

Father, you have called us to a pilgrimage of faith. The light of your truth summons us, and the call of faith is a constant challenge on our journey. We give thanks for the desire to seek you: we give thanks for voices from the past that offer guidance, for signposts pointing to the next stage, for companions who share the journey, for footsteps in the sand of pilgrims before us, for the conviction that, unseen but not unknown, you are with us. Father, keep us faithful to the vision, and steadfast on our pilgrimage so that the distant goal may become a reality, and faith at last lead to sight.

Welsh

> God guide me with thy wisdom,
> God chastise me with thy justice,
> God help me with thy mercy,
> God protect me with thy strength.
>
> God fill me with thy fullness,
> God shield me with thy shade,
> God fill me with thy grace,
> For the sake of thine anointed Son.

114

Jesu Christ of the seed of David,
Visiting One of the Temple,
Sacrificial Lamb of the Garden,
Who died for me.

Carmina Gadelica I, 65

Like grace dripping off the trees
your love pours on us
blessing and wetting us.

It soaks us with joy
and spreads through the blood
of felt passion.

We praise and give thanks
for the desire
and longing to praise.

Forgive our falling and
continue to be our beloved
Companion on the Way.

Blaise Gillespie

BLESS THE LORD,
ALL BIRDS OF
THE AIR,
SING HIS PRAISE
AND EXALT HIM
FOR EVER.

CREATION

BLESS THE LORD,
YOU CATTLE AND
WILD BEASTS,
SING HIS PRAISE
AND EXALT HIM
FOR EVER.

BENEDICITE

CREATION

Almighty Creator,
it is you who have made the land and the sea . . .
The world cannot comprehend in song bright
    and melodious,
even though the grass and trees
should sing, all your wonders,
O true Lord!

The Father created the world by a miracle;
it is difficult to express its measure.
Letters cannot contain it,
letters cannot comprehend it.

Old Welsh (translated by Oliver Davies)

Celtic Christians believed in a God that is Creator 'of all that is, seen and unseen'. They found
the hand of God in all things and as St David
said, we are to value the 'little things' and find
God in them.

The whole approach of Celtic spirituality is
familial, simple and mystical. Mysticism is not
merely about visions and ecstasy, but consists
in living the Christian mystery and being trans-
formed by it. The mystical approach is to find
the extraordinary in the ordinary, to find eternity in the familiar objects we handle and use
every day.

> My Chief of generous heroes, bless
> my loom and all things near to me,
> bless me in my busy-ness,
> keep me for life safe-dear to thee.
> *Trad. Gaelic*

Towards the world round about us we are to have a double-value; we are to value each thing for its specific 'is-ness'.

Celtic spirituality teaches us to become aware that we are in each particular thing: and then in each thing and through each thing we learn to apprehend the presence of the living God. Things that are solid, with sharp outline and distinct relief, are at the same time transparent sacraments of God's presence, and a means of communion with him.

The poet George Herbert wrote, 'Teach me, my God and King, in all things thee to see.' The whole universe is interrelated and interdependent. All matter is connected, a fact acknowledged by both mystic and scientist. All movement, sound, vibration has a repercussion and effect throughout the whole of the created order. The most important heritage which Celtic Christianity received from the old religion was the profound sense of the immanence of God in the world. The Celtic Christians remained very much aware of the divine presence in all of nature: in the elements, in the seasons. It is this sense of an all-pervading presence that is characteristic of their Christian piety.

Through prayer and through blessing the matter of God and its artifacts, the Celt became the mystical bonding between the heavenly and the earthly: between God and his Creation. He became the symbol of creation made conscious of itself; in him immanence and transcendence met. The outward and inward, physical and spiritual, were linked. Through the act of blessing, nature becomes sacrament.

Ocean Blessing

God the Father all-powerful, benign,
Jesu the Son of tears and of sorrow,
With thy co-assistance, O! Holy Spirit.

The Three-One, ever-living, ever-mighty,
 everlasting,
Who brought the Children of Israel through
 the Red Sea,
And Jonah to land from the belly of the great
 creature of the ocean,

Who brought Paul and his companions in the
 ship,
From the torment of the sea, from the dolour
 of the waves,
From the gale that was great, from the storm
 that was heavy.

When the storm poured on the Sea of Galilee ...

Sain* us and shield and sanctify us,
Be Thou, King of the elements, seated at our
 helm,
And lead us in peace to the end of our journey.

With winds mild, kindly, benign, pleasant,
Without swirl, without whirl, without eddy,
That would do no harmful deed to us.

We ask all things of thee, O God,
According to thine own will and word.

Carmina Gadelica I, 329

* To cross oneself as a sign of consecration or
protection.

A Sea Benison

When the sailor from the Western Isles of Scotland had reached port and left the tossing waves behind, he spoke to God this lovely prayer:

Father of Powers, by whose sure guiding
We have cleft the deep,
Now underneath thy brooding wings of love
Grant us the boon of sleep.

Jesus, Lord of the calm, and of the storm,
Whatever seas I sail upon, be
Thou my helm, my compass,
and my port.

Hebridean

Rite of Sprinkling at a Holy Well

The wellspring is a symbol of the basic source of life. The site of many a Celtic saint's dwelling is marked by a holy well to which the saints were often divinely led and from which they derived natural refreshment. Water is necessary for physical survival, as well as for cleanliness, health and comfort; and it is necessary for baptism. The sacramental intermingling of the natural and the supernatural is very much in the Celtic Christian tradition.

In this rite, water is not brought from somewhere and poured in a font: it is living water, springing forth from the ground. Some wells have steps going down like many ancient baptistries, symbolizing that baptism is both a cleansing and going down into the death of Christ, and rising with him in new life. Holy sprinkling is a natural sacramental action, when, by the use of water as a sign and pledge of God's grace, we are enabled to receive inward and spiritual healing.

Prayer:
Graciously hear us, God our Saviour, that as we rejoice in the memory of blessed N (*quote Saint's name in whose memory the well is dedicated*), we may be instructed in the love of a holy life. Through Jesus Christ our Lord.

In the name of the Father, and of the Son, and of the Holy Spirit. Amen.

V. The Lord be with you.

R. And also with you.

Jesus said: 'Come unto me, all you who labour and are overburdened, and I will give you rest. Your heavenly Father knows you have need of all these things.'

Silent Prayer

Let us commend ourselves and each other to the grace and power of Jesus Christ, that the Lord may ease our suffering and grant us health and salvation. To prepare ourselves for this holy sprinkling, let us call to mind our sins.

Lord Jesus, you healed the sick:
Lord, have mercy.
R. Lord, have mercy.

Lord Jesus, you forgave sinners:
Christ, have mercy.
R. Christ, have mercy.

Lord Jesus, you give us yourself to heal us and bring us strength.
Lord, have mercy.
R. Lord, have mercy.

May Almighty God have mercy upon us, forgive us our sins, and bring us to everlasting life. Amen.

Pilgrims normally stand to be sprinkled. They may drink the water, the sign of God's life being given to the soul; the sign of the Cross is made on their forehead in remembrance of their baptism; they may make a cup with their hands and scoop the water in them applying the water to any part of their bodies.

The priest/minister sprinkles the assembled pilgrims saying:

May Almighty God, at the intercession of Saint N, grant you health and peace.

Let us pray:
Lord, in your mercy give us living water, always springing up as a fountain of salvation: free us, body and soul, from every danger and admit us to your presence in purity of heart. Grant this through Christ our Lord. Amen.[6]

Rune of the Well

> The shelter of Mary Mother
> Be nigh my hands and my feet
> To go out to the well
> And to bring me safely home,
> And to bring me safely home.
>
> May warrior Michael aid me,
> May Brigit calm preserve me,
> May sweet Brianag give me light,
> And Mary pure be near me,
> And Mary pure be near me.
>
> *Carmina Gadelica III, 169*

Blessing of Animals

Love all God's creation, the whole of it
and every grain of sand, love every leaf,
every ray of God's light;
love the animals, love the plants,
love everything.
If you love everything, you will perceive
the divine mystery in things.
And once you have perceived it,
you will begin to comprehend it ceaselessly,
more and more every day.
And you will at last come to love the whole
   world
with an abiding, universal love.
Love the animals:
God has given them the rudiments of
   thought
and untroubled joy.
Do not, therefore, trouble it,
Do not torture them,
do not deprive them of their joy,
do not go against God's intent.

Fyodor Mikhailovich Dostoevsky

  Bless the Lord, all birds of the air;
  sing his praise and exalt him for ever.
  Bless the Lord, you cattle and wild beasts;
  sing his praise and exalt him for ever.

  Benedicite

Let us listen to the Word of God:

From the earth the Lord God formed all the wild animals and all the birds of the air, and brought them to the man to see what he would call them; whatever the man called each living creature, that would be its name. The man gave names to all cattle, to the birds of the air and to every wild animal. (Genesis 2:19–20)

Psalm: 148:7–13.

Response: Let all the earth praise the name of the Lord.

1. Praise the Lord from the earth,
   you sea monsters and ocean depths;
   fire and hail, snow and ice,
   gales of wind that obey his voice.
Response

2. All mountains and hills;
   all fruit trees and cedars,
   wild animals and all cattle,
   reptiles and winged birds.
Response

3. Let kings and all peoples,
   princes and all rulers,
   youth and girls together,
   let them praise the name of the Lord.
Response

Let us pray:
Blessed are you, Lord God,
for all living creatures you have made.
You keep them in your care
and not one is lost without your knowing.
They glorify you, each in its own way

and speak to us of your beauty and love.
May we respect them and cherish them
for they are your gift to us;
through them may we come to know you better
and praise you, their Creator.
This we ask through Christ our Lord. Amen.

Roman Ritual

THE PROTECTION OF THE CATTLE

Pastures smooth, long, and spreading,
Grassy meads aneath your feet,
The friendship of God the Son to bring you home
To the field of the fountains,
Field of the fountains.

Closed be every pit to you,
Smoothed be every knoll to you,
Cosy every exposure to you,
Beside the cold mountains,
Beside the cold mountains.

The care of Peter and of Paul,
The care of James and of John,
The care of Bride fair and of Mary Virgin,
To meet you and to tend you,
Oh! The care of all the band
To protect you and to strengthen you.

Carmina Gadelica I, 279

.

MAY HE THAT
PROVIDED
THE SEED
FOR SOWING,
THE HAND
FOR DOING,
THE MIND
FOR THINKING
AND
THE HEART
FOR LOVING,
THE FATHER,
SON AND
HOLY SPIRIT,
BLESS & PRESERVE
YOU ALL THE
DAYS OF YOUR
LIFE.
AMEN

TIMES AND SEASONS

TIMES AND SEASONS

The earth is the creation of the Lord God, and the Lord made it for all his creatures to enjoy. Human beings have the stewardship of it. Yes, God has given us this world to use, to love, to care for, to treasure. How easily we forget what a wonderful treasure this world of ours – and his – is. We must think carefully about what we do to this world we have been given; what we should be doing to keep this treasure in right order, to keep it safe and protected, living and growing.

God is central to his creation and to all human endeavour, especially to that of food production. The blessings and services and prayers in this section therefore praise and give thanks to God for all his goodness; for the beauty and fertility of the earth and for the skills he has given to people to tend his earth.

Food and farming have always aroused religious ritual response and since early times, particularly in the Celtic tradition, praise and thanksgiving have been offered to God. The elements are a very important factor in Celtic countries, and great respect is paid to the Lord of the Elements, as well as to the Lord of the Harvest.

Blessing of the New Year

God bless to me the new day,
Never vouchsafed to me before;
It is to bless thine own presence
Thou hast given me this time, O God.

Bless thou to me mine eye,
May mine eye bless all it sees;
I will bless my neighbour,
May my neighbour bless me.

God, give me a clean heart,
Let me not from sight of thine eye;
Bless to me my children and my wife,
And bless to me my means and my cattle.

Carmina Gadelica I, 159

Plough Blessing

In early times there were Plough Monday cele-
brations, marking a return to work after the
Christmas season. A communal plough often
was kept in church. At the end of the Christmas
season when there was no work, there were, as
a result, no wages nor free meals. The ploughman would take the plough round the farmers
and landowners to beg for silver.

This service for the blessing of the plough
may be used after a homily at the Holy Eucharist. A plough, a large container of soil and perhaps a milk churn may be placed in the church.

PLOUGH SUNDAY BLESSING

The month of May, the ploughman is
    extravagant:
every dyke is shelter to the destitute;
joyful is the lightly clad old man;
the wood is leafy, the wanton is glad;
reconciliation is easy where there is love;
tuneful are the cuckoo and the hound;
not less soon in going to market
is the lamb's skin than the sheep's skin.
Early Welsh

There is a time for working and a time for
    resting,
a time for ploughing and a time for sowing,
a time for dressing and a time for
    harvesting.

There is a time for lambing and a time for
    culling,
a time for the byre, a time for the field,
a time for the market and a time for God.
Indeed all times are his.

BLESSING OF THE SOIL

Farmer: O Lord, all the earth is yours. We
bring before you this rich and living
soil that you may bless it and our
lands with abundant fertility.

Priest or
Minister: In the name of the Creator of heaven
and earth, I bless † this living soil,
that it may produce for those who respect and love it, food in abundance
for birds, beasts and all people.

Let the heavens rejoice and let the earth be
    glad:
Let the field be joyful, and all that is in it.

BLESSING OF THE PLOUGH

Farmer: This plough, whose share turns the
soil, we bring before you, O Lord,
that you may look with favour on all
we do to cultivate the soil.

Priest or
Minister: In the name of the Most High God, I
bless this plough †, and all of you
who work the soil. May the Lord
open the heavens for you, his rich
treasure house to give rain upon

your land at the proper time, and
bless everything to which you turn
your hand. God speed the plough!

May the blessing of God Almighty,
The Father, Son and Holy Spirit,
be upon you and upon all who work upon the
    land,
that all creation may glorify his name.
Amen.

THE CONSECRATION OF THE SEED

I will go out to sow the seed,
In name of him who gave it growth;
I will place my front in the wind,
And throw a gracious handful on high.
Should a grain fall on a bare rock,
It shall have no soil in which to grow;
As much falls into the earth,
The dew will make it to be full.

Friday, day auspicious,
The dew will come down to welcome
Every seed that lay in sleep
Since the coming of cold without mercy;
Every seed will take root in the earth,
As the king of the elements desired,
The braird* will come forth with the dew,
It will inhale life from the soft wind.

I will come round with my step,
I will go rightways with the sun,
In name of Ariel and the angels nine,
In name of Gabriel and the Apostles kind.

* *braird*: the first shoots of corn to sprout.

134

Father, Son, and Spirit Holy,
Be giving growth and kindly substance
To every thing that is in my ground,
Till the day of gladness shall come.

The Feast day of Michael, day beneficent,
I will put my sickle round about
The root of my corn as was wont;
I will lift the first cut quickly;
I will put it three turns round
My head, saying my rune the while,
My back to the airt* of the north;
My face to the fair sun of power.

I shall throw the handful far from me,
I shall close my two eyes twice,
Should it fall in one bunch
My stacks will be productive and lasting;
No Carlin will come with bad times
To ask a palm bannock‡ from us,
What time rough storms come with frowns
Nor stint nor hardship shall be on us.

Carmina Gadelica I, 243

---

* *airt*: a quarter of the compass.
‡ *bannock*: a round, flat cake, usually made of oat-meal.

135

Spring

V.   My song shall be always of the loving kindness of the Lord.

R.   With my mouth will I ever be sharing your
truth from generation to generation.

Raw and chilly is icy spring,
cold will arise in the wind;
the ducks of the watery pool are crying,
eager is the harsh-shrieking crane.
Wolves hear in the wilderness
the early rise of morning time;
birds awaken from islands,
many are the wild creatures from which they
    flee
out of the wood, out of the green grass.

Eleventh-century Irish

Reading:

The Lord will love you, bless you, and increase
your numbers. He will bless the fruit of your
soil, your grain and new wine and oil, the
young of your herds and lambing flocks, in the
land which he swore to your forefathers he
would give you. (Deuteronomy 7:13)

Prayer:

Lord,
You are always more ready to hear than we to
    pray;
you give us more than we desire or deserve.
Show us your mercy;

forgive us those things of which our
    conscience is afraid,
and grant us those things for which we can
    ask only
through the intercession of Jesus Christ, your
    Son. Amen.

Welsh Book of Common Prayer

Blessing:
May the Lord of the Spring bless pastures and
    meadows, †
all growing things, grass and green fields.
May they remain healthy and unspoilt,
and be devoted to the greater glory of
    creation.
Amen.

The Beltane Blessing

Beltane is the first day of May. This blessing was given for protection of all living things during the forthcoming year.

All fires were extinguished and a new fire would be kindled, usually on a knoll or hill. This fire was then divided into two and humans and animals would leap over it or run through it for purification.

Bless, O Threefold true and bountiful,
Myself, my spouse, and my children,
My tender children and their beloved mother
   at their head.
On the fragrant plain, on the gay mountain
   sheiling,
On the fragrant plain, on the gay mountain
   sheiling.

Everything within my dwelling or in my
   possession,
All kine and crops, all flocks and corn,
From Hallow Eve to Beltane Eve,
With goodly progress and gentle blessing,
From sea to sea, and every river mouth,
From wave to wave, and base of waterfall.

Be the Three Persons taking possession of all
   to me belonging,
Be the sure Trinity protecting me in truth;
Oh! Satisfy my soul in the words of Paul,
And shield my loved ones beneath the wing of
   thy glory,

Shield my loved ones beneath the wing of thy
   glory.

Bless everything and every one,
Of this little household by my side;
Place the cross of Christ on us with the power
   of love,
Till we see the land of joy,
Till we see the land of joy.

What time the kine shall forsake the stalls,
What time the sheep shall forsake the folds,
What time the goats shall ascend to the mount
   of mist,
May the tending of the Triune follow them,
May the tending of the Triune follow them.

Thou Being who didst create me at the
   beginning,
Listen and attend me as I bend the knee to
   thee,
Morning and evening as is becoming in me,
In thine own presence, O God of life,
In thine own presence, O God of life.

Carmina Gadelica I, 183

Blessing for Fishing

A traditional prayer of blessing of the River Teifi, Cardiganshire, and an invocation for the bounty of the season's sewin (salmon trout) fishing.

This prayer has been offered up locally by all accounts since 1900 and follows the tradition of St Dogmael's Abbey, Ceredigion, where the Abbot would give his annual blessing for the harvest of the waters from a great granite slab which originally lay in mud close to the ancient net pool. The stone remains to this day. Fishermen traditionally offered the first of the catch to the Abbey in the vain hope that the monks would thereafter keep their distance as the sight of a black or white robe was seen in the same light as an albatross.

Almighty and bountiful God, who brought
    together the waters
and did'st separate them from the land,
and opened up the Red Sea that thy people
    Israel
may pass through their midst,
and did'st thyself walk upon the waters;
who silenced the raging of the sea
and by whose bountiful grace filled the nets of
    the disciples;
grant we beseech thee, that the harvest of this
    fervent stream
may be safely gathered in.
Defend each fisherman and sailor from the
    perils of the deep

that they in this life, having reaped the bounty
of their good labour, may at the last return
   home
to the haven of eternal life.
And may the blessing and peace of Almighty
   God,
Father, Son and Holy Spirit, descend upon
   these blessed waters
and all who wander the ways of the seas.
Amen.

Translated from the original Welsh text by Ian Foster

Rogationtide
(the Fifth Sunday after Easter)

The words in the Prayer Book Gospel for the day begin: 'Whatever you ask the Father in my name, he will give to you.' (From the Latin *rogare* – to ask.)

Originally, Rogation Days were held on the Monday, Tuesday and Wednesday before Ascension Day. In the Western Church, processions to bless the crops, and later to include 'beating the bounds', developed from the old Roman rites of *Robigalia* (from the Latin *robigo*, for 'rust' or 'mould'), when prayers would be offered to the deity for crops to be spared from mildew. It is no coincidence that today, farmers now spray their crops against mildew.

The Blessing used here is suitable for use in church; however, processions or walks may be conducted in the manner of 'living walking', as George Herbert puts it. Separate blessings are added for that purpose at the end of the church service, and may be inserted into the liturgy at the place indicated.

ROGATIONTIDE BLESSING SERVICE

The month of June, beautiful are the lands,
the sea is smooth, the strands are gay,
long and fair is the day, women are lively.
The flock is abundant, the bogs are passable;
God loves all peace,
the devil causes all mischief;

everyone desires honour;
the strong comes to a feeble end.

Early Welsh

While the earth endures seed time and harvest, cold and heat, summer and winter, day and night, shall not cease. (Genesis 8:22)

There is a time for working and time for
    resting,
a time for ploughing and a time for sowing,
a time for spraying and a time for harvesting,
there is a time for lambing and a time for
    culling,
there is a time for the byre, a time for the
    field,
and a time for the market, and a time for God.
Indeed all times are his.

V.   The heavens are yours and the earth is
     also yours.
R.   You have laid the foundations of the round
     world and all that is in it.

THE BLESSING

Seeds we bring: we ask you to bless them, Lord.

Fields we bring: we ask you to bless them, Lord.

Gardens we bring: we ask you to bless them, Lord.

Lambs we bring: we ask you to bless them, Lord.

Calves we bring: we ask you to bless them, Lord.

Priest or
Minister: In the name of the Lord I bless † them for human use and in their own goodness. May they be a blessing to us, material and spiritual; may we who care for them and enjoy them reap material and spiritual fruit.

COVENANT OF RECONCILIATION

Minister: Brothers and sisters, we covenant today with one another:
All: With every living creature and all on which we depend.

With all that is on earth and with earth itself.

With all that lives in the waters and with the waters themselves.

With all the creatures of the air, and with the air itself.

With all that is warm with life, and with the living fire.

We commit ourselves today to put away all selfishness and greed and to embrace one another in love and joy and peace.

May he that provided the seed for sowing,
the hand for doing,
the mind for thinking
and the heart for loving,
the Father, Son and Holy Spirit,
bless and preserve you all the days of your life.
Amen.

*At this point a procession may leave the church
and walks the bounds*

Blessing in a position facing fields and gardens

Prayer:
Creator Spirit,
Who broods everlastingly over the lands and
    waters,
Who endows them with forms and colours
which no human skill can copy:
give us today, we ask you,
the mind and heart to rejoice in your creation.
Amen.

Blessing:
Almighty God,
Whose will it is that the earth should bear its
    fruits in their seasons:
bless the labours of those who work in the
    field,
bless the increase of crops and grain and fruit-
    bearing trees,
that bread and wine and wholesome food
may be shared and enjoyed by all your people.
Amen.

Blessing in a position facing animals, birds and other creatures

Prayer:
O Lord, who surrounds with your love all
    things living,
and promises to save both man and beast:
We thank you for the companionship of
    animals and birds,
without which there would be for humankind
a great loneliness of spirit on the earth.
When we are careless of the beasts
and forget that they are your creatures,
forgive us.
Amen.

Blessing:
May God's blessing shower upon all his
    creatures;
may peace pervade the whole creation;
may there be an abundance of plants we use;
may humankind prosper and animals flourish.
Bless all living things, O Lord.

Blessing in a position facing the houses of the village (or town)

Prayer:
Help us with your grace, good Lord, to live as true followers of your Son Jesus Christ:

V.   Lord in your mercy,
R.   Hear our prayer.

That in all things we may hold to your will and purpose:

V.   Lord in your mercy,
R.   Hear our prayer.

That our hearts and minds may be open to your holiness and truth:

V.   Lord in your mercy,
R.   Hear our prayer.

That we may rightly value the whole of your creation:

V.   Lord in your mercy,
R.   Hear our prayer.

That we may seek your righteousness in all our dealings with one another:

V.   Lord in your mercy,
R.   Hear our prayer.

That we may bear each other's burdens, and so obey your law:

V.   Lord in your mercy,
R.   Hear our prayer.

That in all our time on earth we may work and live as citizens of your heavenly kingdom: Grant this, O Lord.

Blessing:
God bless this village (parish or town),
its farmers, its houses and its people.
May he visit you with his mercy,
surround you with his love
and make you perfect to do his will.
Amen.

Suggested Hymn:
(to be sung while people return or on return to church)

All creatures of our God and King . . .

Summer

V. Let his whole creation bless the Lord,
R. Sing his praise and exalt him for ever.

Summer has come, healthy and free,
at which the dark wood becomes bowed:
the slender nimble deer leaps
when the path of seals is smooth.

The cuckoo sings sweet soft music
at which there is tranquil unbroken sleep.
Gentle birds hop about the knoll
and swift grey stags.

Heat has laid hold on the repose of the deer.
Pleasant is the cry of active packs;
the white stretch of the strand smiles
where the brisk sea is turbulent.

The noise of the wanton winds in the top
of the dark oakwood of Drum Daill:
the noble hornless herd runs
to which Cuan Wood is a shelter.

Green bursts out on every plant,
wooded is the copse of the green oak-grove;
summer has come, winter has gone,
tangled hollies wound the hound.

The hardy blackbird sings a strain,
to whom the thorny wood is a heritage.
The sad turbulent sea is sleeping,
the speckled salmon leaps.

The sun smiles over every land.
I am freed from the brood of winter,

hounds bark, stags assemble,
ravens flourish, summer has come.

Early Irish (translated by Kenneth Jackson)

Prayer:

Almighty God, who has blessed the earth that it should be fruitful and bring forth abundantly what is needed for the life of humankind: bless, we pray thee, the labour of all who cultivate and harvest the land, and bless with such seasonable weather that we may gather in the fruits of the earth and ever rejoice in thy goodness, to the praise of thy holy Name; through Jesus Christ our Lord, Amen.

From the Welsh

Lammas Blessing
(Stewardship Sunday)

Lammas (1 August) is the time of first fruits, the first reward of the tilling, the sowing and the tending. The corn harvest is much earlier today than it used to be because of the predominance of winter sowing. August is also a popular time for holidays. Underlying the Lammas practices of offering the first fruits is the recognition that this is God's world; if we are to enjoy it and live in it according to his way, we do well not to keep the best for ourselves. It is another way of affirming that God comes first. The Sunday nearest to Lammas could be designated Stewardship Sunday.

Along with the Harvest Festival, this is the most biblical of the agricultural festivals. A parallel can be made with the Feast of the First Fruits in the Old Testament. Thus the custom of offering the first and best of the corn, new wine and oil, flocks and fleece was easily absorbed into the Christian tradition. For some the offering of the first loaf, probably barley bread, or lamb, or a late cut of hay (if the fields had to be grazed earlier in the year) was appropriate. The terms Loaf-mass, Lamb-mass or Latter-mass reflect these variations. In Old Testament times the offering went to the priests for their living. Often in the Middle Ages, rents were paid at this time or feudal tributes of land were made. Also it was customary to consecrate bread from the first cut ripe corn at

Mass on 1 August (not necessarily a Sunday) in thanksgiving for the harvest.

LAMMAS SERVICE OF BLESSING

The month of August, the salt-marsh is full of
   snails,
the bees are merry, the hive is full;
the work of the sickle is better than that of
   the bow;
the rick is more frequent than the playing-field;
who works not nor prays,
he does not deserve his bread;
Saint Brenda spoke truth –
'Evil is sought after no less than the good.'
Early Welsh

Sentence:
When you come into the land which I give you
and reap its harvest, you shall bring the sheaf
of the first fruits of your harvest to the priest.
(Leviticus 23:10)

Readings (suggested):

Old Testament:	Deuteronomy 18:1–5
	Ezekiel 34:11–24
New Testament:	Matthew 15:32–39
	2 Peter 1:1–11

Reaping Blessing

On Tuesday of the feast at the rise of the sun,
and the back of the ear of corn to the east,
I will go forth with my sickle under my arm,
and I will reap the cut the first act.

I will let my sickle down
While the fruitful ear is in my grasp,
I will raise mine eye upwards,
I will turn me on my heel quickly,

Rightway as travels the sun
From the airt* of the east to the west,
From the airt of the north with motion calm
To the very core of the airt of the south.

I will give thanks to the King of grace
For the growing crops of the ground,
He will give food to ourselves and to the flocks
According as he disposeth to us.

James and John, Peter and Paul,
Mary beloved, the fullness of light,
On Michaelmas Eve and Christmas,
We will all taste of the bannock.

Carmina Gadelica I, 249

Intercessions may be made and first fruits from field and garden may be offered. The following type of declaration could be made, for example:

---

* *airt*: a quarter of the compass.

Offertory:

A strawberry I bring, a choice fruit from my crop *

A cabbage I bring, the best I have *

A cake I bring, the best that I could bake *

I bring the best that I could buy * *(a purchase from a shop).*

* *Different people present and in this way make appropriate offerings.*

We offer this loaf which represents bread made from this year's grain. Will you bless it and all we grow to our use?

Priest or
Minister: May God bless you in all your growing and cropping.
May he bless you in the fruit of the field and the fruit of the garden.
(May you enjoy the blessing of the Bread of Life.
May you find life in the Lamb who died and was raised to life.)

Final Blessing *(perhaps after communion)*:
May he whose earth and sun and turning year brought the first fruits to ripeness,
the Father, the Son and the Holy Spirit,
bless you and preserve you all the days of your life. Amen.

Harvest Blessing
(September or October)

Of the four agricultural festivals, Plough, Rogation, Lammas and Harvest, Harvest is the one
that remains a popular occasion in town and
country. It has gathered to itself elements of
the others. A popular hymn such as 'We plough
the fields and scatter ...' speaks of the ploughing, sowing and the increase, and the harvest
of weeds as well as crops. We also commonly
speak of offering the first and the best. If Harvest is seen as one of a cycle of four, then the
strongest specific emphasis will be on comple-
tion. All is safely gathered in.

The month of September, there is verse in the
    Canon,
the ripening season of corn and fruit;
woe to my heart for longing;
the eye of God is upon the poor;
the worst privilege is the insulting of people,
the worst good is through perjury;
arrogance and oppression of the innocent
are the ruin of heirs.

Early Welsh

Sentence:
The earth is the Lord's and all that is in it. The
compass of the world and those that dwell in it.
(Psalm 24:1)

*Harvest gifts may be brought forward now or at a
later point in the service. This format is useful in*

*a Harvest Communion after the Gospel and hom-
ily. The gifts and collection are dedicated.*

Loving Father, we thank you for your gifts and
kindness to us. Give us the right spirit to use
properly what you provide in Jesus' name.
Amen.

Prayer:
There is a time for working and a time for
    resting,
a time for ploughing and a time for sowing,
a time for dressing and a time for harvesting,
there is a time for lambing and a time for
    culling,
a time for the byre and a time for the market,
there is also a time greatly to be longed for,
when all is completed and God is all in all.

Intercessions and petitions

Prayer:
Lord of all creation.
You give us the fruits of the earth in their
    season.
Help us to receive them gratefully and to use
    them wisely in your service;
through Jesus Christ our Lord. Amen.

Blessing:
Blessing and honour, thanksgiving and praise
more than we can utter be unto you,
most adorable Trinity,
Father, Son and Holy Spirit
by all angels, all people, all creatures,

for ever and ever.
Amen.

To God the Father, who first loved us,
and made us accepted in the Beloved,
To God the Son who loved us,
and washed us from our sins in his own blood;
To God the Holy Spirit,
who sheds the love of God abroad in our
  hearts
be all love and all glory
for time and eternity.
Amen.

Autumn

While the earth remains, seedtime and harvest, cold and heat, summer and winter, day and night, shall not cease. (Genesis 8:22)

A good tranquil season is Autumn;
there is occupation then for everyone
throughout the very short days.
Dappled fawns from the side of the hinds,
the red stalks of the bracken shelter them;
stags run from knolls
at the belling of the deer-herd.

Sweet acorns in the high woods,
corn-stalks about cornfields
over the expanse of the brown earth.
Prickly thorn-bushes of the bramble
by the midst of the ruined court:
the hard ground is covered with heavy fruit.
Hazelnuts of good crop fall
from the huge old trees of mounds.

Eleventh-century Irish

Bless the Lord, all that grows in the earth;
sing his praise and exalt him for ever.

Benedicite

Prayer:
Almighty and everlasting God, who crownest the year with thy goodness, and hast given to us the fruits of the earth in their season, give us, we beseech thee, grateful hearts, that we may rightly use thy gifts to thy glory; through Jesus Christ our Lord. Amen.

Winter

Winter has come with scantiness,
lakes have flooded the land,
frosts crumble the leaves,
the merry wave mutters.

Early Irish

Keen is the wind, bare the hill, it is difficult to
    find shelter,
the ford is marred, the lake freezes,
a man could stand on a single stalk.

Wave after wave covers the shore;
very loud are the outcries before the heights
    of the hill;
scarcely can one stand outside.

Gold is the bed of the lake before the tumult of
    winter,
the reeds are withered, the stalks are broken,
the wind is boisterous, the wood is bare.

Cold is the bed of the fish in the shelter of the ice,
thin is the stag, the grass is bearded,
short is the evening, the trees are bowed.

Early Welsh

Bless the Lord, sleet and falling snow;
sing his praise and exalt him for ever.
Bless the Lord, frost and cold;
sing his praise and exalt him for ever.
Let the earth bless the Lord,
sing his praise and exalt him for ever.

Benedicite

Prayer:

May he that provided the seasons of the year for the well-being of all created things, who gave us a time for working and a time for resting, a time for ploughing and a time for sowing, a time for culling and a time for harvesting, a time for the field and time for God, bless and preserve us for evermore in the Name of the Father, † the Son and the Holy Spirit. Amen.

May the Lord bless us, keep us from all evil and lead us to everlasting life. Amen.

Christmas Chant

Hail King! Hail King! Blessed is he! Blessed is
  he!
Hail King! Hail King! Blessed is he! Blessed is
  he!
Ho, hail! Blessed the King!
Ho, hi! Let there be joy!

Prosperity be upon this dwelling,
On all that ye have heard and seen,
On the bare bright floor flags,
On the shapely standing stone staves,
Hail King! Hail King! Blessed is he! Blessed is
  he!

Bless this house and all that it contains,
From rafter and stone and beam;
Deliver it to God from pall to cover,
Be the healing of men therein,
Hail King! Hail King! Blessed is he! Blessed is
  he!

Be ye in lasting possession of the house,
Be ye healthy about the hearth,
Many be the ties and stakes in the homestead,
People dwelling on this foundation,
Hail King! Hail King! Blessed is he! Blessed is
  he!

Offer to the Being from found to cover,
Include stave and stone and beam;
Offer again both rods and cloth,
Be health to the people therein,
Hail King! Hail King! Blessed is he! Blessed is
  he!

Hail King! Hail King! Blessed is he! Blessed is
  he!
Ho, hail! Blessed the King!
Let there be joy!

Blessed the King,
Without beginning, without ending,
To everlasting, to eternity,
Every generation for aye,
Ho! Hi! Let there be joy!

Carmina Gadelica I, 135

HOLY CHRIST,
BLESS ME WITH
    THY PRESENCE
WHEN MY DAYS
 ARE WEARY AND
    MY FRIENDS
    FEW.
    BLESS ME WITH THY PRESENCE
        WHEN MY JOY IS FULL,
        LEST I FORGET

PRAYER
AND WORSHIP

THE GIVER OF
THE GIFT.
BLESS ME
WITH THY
PRESENCE
WHEN I SHALL
MAKE AN END OF LIVING.
HELP ME IN THE DARKNESS
TO FIND THE FORD ✛ AND IN MY
GOING, COMFORT ME WITH THY
PROMISE THAT WHERE
THOU ART, THERE SHALL
    THY SERVANT BE

HEBRIDEAN BLESSING

PRAYER AND WORSHIP

Question: And what is the fruit of study?

Answer: To perceive the eternal Word of God reflected in every plant and insect, every bird and animal, and every man and woman.

Ninian's Catechism

The Christian life, as the Celtic Christian saw it, was for contemplating and practising the presence of God.

The constant remembrance of God gave greater bliss than any worldly pleasure and earthly fulfilment. 'Taste and see', said Columbanus recalling Psalm 34:8, 'how lovely and pleasant is the Lord.' This was the language of the mystic, yet this experience is within the scope of us all.

The modern Welsh poet Rhydwen Williams sees this experience as

> weaving a psalm
> to the unutterable Word
> which dwells in the dewdrop and
> the rock.[7]

For the Celts, the Word of God was a word to be experienced both intellectually and physically. It was to be loved and enjoyed as being the expression of God in nature as much as in the Gospels and Psalms. Celtic clerics and monks constantly recited the Psalter; they loved its poetry and ruminated on it daily. They invented the 'pocket gospels' – manuals of illuminated gospel writing which they kept in leather book scrips (sic) or satchels to be hung by the privileged in their cells. These scholars wrote commentaries on the scriptures, manuals, service books, litanies, blessings and lives of the saints for edification.

The Blessing of a Cross or Crucifix and the Blessing of an Article for Devotional Use are self-explanatory. The section of Ancient and Modern Celtic Blessings may be used for post-Eucharistic or other sacramental use. The blessings may also be used in the spirit of the early Celtic Christians and Desert Fathers who read for savour, not science. For them the Holy Scripture was a well from which to draw, the waters of which would be poured out in prayer and blessing.

These blessings beg to be read meditatively, in order that God may be met through the sound of sacred words. The Christian Celt did not need to set aside a special period for contemplative prayer. To commune with God all he or she needed to do was to pronounce the word slowly and prayerfully so that the sentence would be heard with the ear of the heart. This word remains for ever:

The word of the Lord remains forever.
What is this Word?
It is the Good News that has been brought to
    you.

1 Peter 1:25

Blessing of a Cross
or Crucifix

V.   Our help is in the name of the Lord.
R.   Who has made both heaven and earth.

V.   The Lord be with you.
R.   And also with you.

Let us pray:
We ask you, Holy Lord, Almighty Father, eternal God: that worthily blessed † this cross may be a sign of the healing of humankind; the affirmation of faith, perfection of good works and the redemption of souls. May it be a comfort, consolation and protection against all evil, Amen.

Bless † O Lord Jesus Christ this cross, through which you have freed the world from the power of evil.

Here holy water may be sprinkled on the cross.

May this crucifix be blessed with the Sign of the Cross in the name of the Father †, and of the Son †, and of the Holy Spirit †; and we pray that all who turn towards God before this cross may find healing of body, mind and spirit. Through the same Christ our Lord. Amen.

Blessing of an Article for Devotional Use

V. The Lord be with you.
R. And also with you.

Let us listen to the word of the Lord:

Be careful not to parade your religion before others; if you do, no reward awaits you with your Father in heaven. So, when you give alms, do not announce it with a flourish of trumpets, as the hypocrites do in synagogues and in the streets to win the praise of others. Truly I tell you they have their reward already. But when you give, do not let your left hand know what your right is doing; your good deed must be secret, and your Father who see what is done in secret will reward you. (Matthew 6:5–6)

Psalm: 48:9–14.
Response: Great is the Lord and most worthy of praise in the city of our God.

1. God, within your temple
   we meditate on your steadfast love.
   God, the praise your name deserves
   is heard at earth's farthest bounds.
Response

2. Your right hand is full of victory.
   The hill of Zion rejoices
   and Judah's cities are glad,
   for you redress their wrongs.
Response

3. Go round Zion in procession,
   count the number of her towers,
   take note of her ramparts,
   pass her palaces in review,
   that you may tell generations yet to come
   that such is God,
   our God for ever;
   He will be our guide for evermore.
Response

Let us pray:
God, by whose Word all being is blessed, pour forth your blessing † upon this object of your creation and upon all who may use it in accordance with your will and towards the glorification of your Holy Name. May we use it as an aid to sincere and devoted prayer. May we continue to grow in prayer and be pleasing to you in our lives. All praise and glory are yours Father, through Christ our Saviour, in the Holy Spirit, God, for ever and ever. Amen.[8]

Ancient and Modern
Celtic Blessings

May the grace of the Lord Jesus sanctify us and
    keep us from all evil;
may he drive far from us all hurtful things,
and purify both our souls and bodies;
may he bind us to himself by the bond of love,
and may his peace abound in our hearts.

Gregorian Sacramentary, sixth century

Christ our God, who art thyself the fulfilment of
    the law and the prophets,
and didst fulfil all the ordered purpose of the
    Father,
always fill our heart with joy and gladness,
now and for ever, world without end,

Liturgy of John Chrysostom and Basil the Great

The Lord bless us, and preserve us from all evil,
and bring us to everlasting life;
and may the souls of the faithful,
through the mercy of God, rest in peace.

Sarum Primer

May the infinite and glorious Trinity,
the Father, the Son, and Holy Spirit,
direct our life in good works,
and after our journey through this world,
grant us eternal rest with the saints.

Mozarabic Liturgy, seventh century

Thou knowest my heart Lord,
that whatsoever thou hast given to thy
   servant,
I desire to spend wholly on thy people
and to consume it all in their service.
Grant unto me then, O Lord my God,
that thine eyes may be opened upon them day
   and night.
Tenderly spread thy care to protect them.
Stretch forth thy holy right hand to bless
   them.
Pour into their hearts thy Holy Spirit
who may abide with them while they pray,
to refresh them with devotion and penitence,
to stimulate them with hope,
to make them humble with fear,
and to inflame them with charity.
May he, the kind Consoler,
succour them in temptation
and strengthen them in all the tribulations of
   this life.

Aelred, 1109–1167

May the road rise to meet you,
May the wind be always at your back,
May the sun shine warm upon your face,
May the rains fall softly upon your fields.
Until we meet again,
May God hold you in the hollow of his hand.

Source unknown (Celtic)

Our Lord Jesus Christ be near thee to defend
   thee,
within thee to refresh thee,
around thee to preserve thee,

before thee to guide thee,
behind thee to justify thee,
above thee to bless thee,
who liveth and reigneth with the Father and
    the Holy Ghost,
God for evermore.

Source unknown

The palmful of the God of life
The palmful of the Christ of Love
The palmful of the Spirit of Peace
Triune of Grace.

Source unknown (Early Scottish)

Deep peace, pure white of the moon to you.
Deep peace, pure green of the grass to you.
Deep peace, pure brown of the earth to you.
Deep peace, pure grey of the dew to you.
Deep peace, pure blue of the sky to you.
Deep peace of the running wave to you.
Deep peace of the flowing air to you.
Deep peace of the quiet earth to you.
Deep peace of the shining stars to you.
Deep peace of the Son of Peace to you.

Fiona Macleod (1855–1905)

May the Creator bless you and keep you,
May the beloved companion face you and have
    mercy upon you;
May the eternal Spirit's countenance be
    turned to you and give you peace;
May the Three in One bless you.

Hebridean

I bless you in the Name of the Father, the Son,
and the Sacred Spirit,
the One and the Three.
May God give you to drink of his cup;
may the sun be bright upon you,
may the night call down peace
and when you come to his household
may the door be open wide for you to go in to
    your joy.

Celtic Daily Prayer[9]

Go in peace:
The Wisdom of the Wonderful Counsellor guide
    you,
The Strength of the Mighty God uphold you,
The love of the Everlasting Father enfold you,
The Peace of the Prince of Peace be upon you.

And the blessing of God,
Father, Son and Holy Spirit,
be upon you all this night and for evermore.

Armenian Orthodox dismissal

May the King shield you in the valleys,
May Christ aid you on the mountains,
May the Spirit bathe you on the slopes,
In hollow, on hill, on plain,
Mountain, valley and plain,
May the Three in One bless you . . .

Hebridean

> May God give us light to guide us,
> courage to support us,
> and love to unite us,
> now and evermore.
>
> *Source unknown*

May the Lord bless you and protect you.
May the Lord smile on you and show you his favour.
May the Lord befriend you and prosper you.

Source unknown

May the love of the Father enfold us,
the wisdom of the Son enlighten us,
the fire of the Spirit enflame us;
and may the blessing of the triune God rest upon us,
and abide with us, now and evermore.

Source unknown

A Weaving Pattern

> The weaving of peace be thine
> Peace around thy soul entwine
> Peace of the Father flowing free
> Peace of the Son sitting over thee
> Peace of the Spirit for me and thee
> Peace of the One
> Peace of the Three
> A weaving of peace be upon thee.
> Around thee twine the Three
> The One and the Trinity
> The Father bind his love
> The Son tie his salvation
> The Spirit wrap his power
> Make you a new creation
> Around thee twine the Three
> The encircling of the Trinity.

David Adam[10]

May Christ's holy, healing, enabling Spirit be
  with you
and guide you on your way at every change
  and turn;
and the blessing . . .

Patterns for Worship

May the God of hope fill us
with all joy and peace in believing,
Through the power of the Holy Spirit,
Amen.

Patterns for Worship

May the Light that shows the Way illuminate
  the mind,
May the Love that knows the Truth unfold
  within the heart,
May the Power that gives true Life arise
  within the soul,
Let Light and Love and Power raise all in
  Christ to God.

The Omega Invocation

May the God of patience and of consolation
grant us to live together after the pattern of
our Lord Jesus Christ, so that with one heart
and one voice we may give glory to God, the
Father of our Lord Jesus Christ. Amen.

Taizé

May our Lord Jesus Christ himself, and God our
Father who has loved us, and given us by his
grace eternal consolation and joyful hope,

comfort our hearts and strengthen them in every good word and work. Amen.

Taizé

May the Lord bless us, the Maker of heaven and earth. Amen.

Taizé

May the love of the Lord Jesus draw you to
    himself:
May the power of the Lord Jesus strengthen
    you in his service.
May the joy of the Lord Jesus fill your spirit,
And the blessing of God Almighty, the Father,
The Son and the Holy Spirit, be upon you
And remain with you for ever. Amen.

World Council of Churches

See that ye be at peace among yourselves, my
    children
And love one another.
Follow the example of good men of old
And God will comfort you and help you,
Both in this world
And in the world which is to come.

Celtic Daily Prayer

May the God of hope fill us with all joy and all peace in believing, that we may be overflowing with hope through the power of the Holy Spirit. Amen.

Taizé

May the God of peace sanctify us wholly, keeping us blameless in body, mind and soul for the coming of our Lord Jesus Christ. Amen.

Taizé

May the Lord bless us and keep us;
May Christ smile upon us and give us his
    grace;
May he unveil his face to us and bring us his
    peace. Amen.

Taizé

The blessing of the God of Sarah and of
    Abraham,
The blessing of the Son, born of Mary,
The blessing of the Holy Spirit who broods
    over us
as a mother over her children,
be with you all. Amen.

St Hilda Community[11]

The Lord bless thee, and keep thee:
the Lord make his face to shine upon thee, and
    be gracious unto thee:
the Lord lift up his countenance upon thee,
    and give thee peace.
(Numbers 6:24–26)

Aaronic blessing

Blessed is he who does good to others and
desires not that others should do good to him.

Brother Giles. From 'The Little Flowers of St. Francis'

May the power and the mystery go before us,
    to show us the way,
shine above us to lighten our world,

lie beneath us to bear us up,
walk with us and give us companionship,
and glow and flow within us to bring us joy.
Amen.[12]

May the God who dances in creation,
who embraces us with human love,
who shakes our lives like thunder,
bless us and drive us out with power
to fill the world with her justice. Amen.

> The blessing of God,
> the eternal goodwill of God,
> the shalom of God,
> the wildness and the warmth of God,
> be among us and between us
> now and always. Amen.

May Holy Wisdom,
kind to humanity,
steadfast, sure and free,
the breath of the power of God;
may she who makes all things new, in every age,
enter our souls,
and make us friends of God,
through Jesus Christ. Amen.

> Now may every living being,
> young or old,
> living near or far,
> known to us or unknown,
> living, departed or yet to be born,
> may every living being
> be full of bliss.
> Amen.

For God's Protection

May the strength of God pilot us.
May the power of God preserve us.
May the wisdom of God instruct us.
May the hand of God protect us.
May the way of God direct us.
May the shield of God defend us.
May the host of God guard us
against the snares of the evil one
and the temptations of the world.
May Christ be with us
Christ above us
Christ in us
Christ before us.
may thy salvation O Lord,
be always ours
this day and for evermore.
Amen.

Hebridean

The circle of Jesus keep you from sorrow
The circle of Jesus today and tomorrow
The circle of Jesus your foes confound
The circle of Jesus your life surround.

The Father on you his blessing bestow
The Son his love towards you flow
The Spirit his presence to you show
On you and all the folk you know
On you and all who around you go
The Threefold blessing may you know.

The joy of this day be yours
The joy of this week be yours
The joy of this year be yours
The joy of the Father be yours

The joy of the Spirit be yours
The joy of the Son be yours
Joy for ever and ever be yours.

The hands of the Father uphold you
The hands of the Saviour enfold you
The hands of the Spirit surround you
And the blessing of God Almighty
Father, Son and Holy Spirit
Uphold you evermore.

David Adam[13]

The Father of many resting places grant you
    rest;
The Christ who stilled the storm grant you
    calm;
The Spirit who fills all things grant you peace,
God's light be your light,
God's love be your love.
God's way be your way.
And the blessing . . .

David Adam[14]

Throughout the day, the good God encompass
  you;
Throughout the night, the saving God enfold
    you;
Throughout your life, the loving God behold
    you.
And the blessing . . .

David Adam

    God show you the way of peace
    that you may receive peace,
    that you may give peace,

that you may live peace,
that you may share peace,
that the peace of God shine in you.
God be with you to guide you,
God be with you to protect you,
God be with you to strengthen you.
God be above you to uplift you,
God be beneath you to support you.
And the blessing of God almighty,
The Father, the Son and the Holy Spirit,
Be with you, and remain with you,
Now and always.

David Adam

In the full tide of the day and in its ebbing,
In the rising of the sun and its setting,
The mighty God be with you
The loving God protect you
The holy God guide you.
And the blessing ...

David Adam

The Lord who conquered darkness with light,
give peace to you.
The Lord who conquered death with life,
give peace to you.
The Lord who conquered loneliness with love,
give peace to you.

David Adam

Bless, O Chief of generous chiefs,
Ourselves and everything anear us,
Bless us in all our actions,
Make thou us safe for ever,
Make us safe for ever ...

Carmina Gadelica I, 31

God of the heights protect and uplift you;
Christ of the depths uphold and sustain you;
Spirit of the slopes guide you and grasp you.

The arm of God be about you,
The way of Christ guide you,
The strength of the Spirit support you.

God be with you on the smooth paths;
Christ be with you in the storms;
The Spirit be with you at all times.

The holy God encircle you and keep you safe;
The mighty God defend you from all dangers;
The loving God give you his peace.

Pray for peace
Speak of peace
Think of peace
Act in peace,
And the peace of the Lord
be always with you.

The Creator who brought order out of chaos,
give peace to you.
The Saviour who stilled the raging storm,
give peace to you.
The Spirit who broods on the deeps,
give peace to you.

God grant you peace,
to achieve peace
to radiate peace
to extend peace
to live in peace.

David Adam[15]

The blessing of God and the Lord be yours,
The blessing of the perfect Spirit be yours,
The blessing of the Three be pouring for you
Mildly and generously,
Mildly and generously.[16]

The eye of the great God be upon you,
The eye of the God of glory be on you,
The eye of the Son of Mary Virgin be on you,
The eye of the Spirit mild be on you,
To aid you and to shepherd you;
Oh the kindly eye of the Three be on you,
To aid you and to shepherd you.

May the everlasting Father Himself take you
In his own generous clasp,
In his own generous arm.

May God shield you on every steep,
May Christ keep you in every path,
May Spirit bathe you in every pass.

May the everlasting Father shield you
East and west wherever you go.

May Christ's safeguard protect you ever.

May God make safe to you each steep,
May God make open to you each pass,
May God make clear to you each road,
And may he take you in the clasp of his own
    two hands.

Oh may each saint and sainted woman in
    heaven,
God of the creatures and God of good news,
Be taking charge of you in every strait
Every side and every turn you go.

Be each saint in heaven.
Each sainted woman in heaven,
Each angel in heaven
Stretching their arms for you,
Smoothing the way for you,
When you go thither
Over the river hard to see;
Oh when you go thither home
Over the river hard to see.

May the Father take you
In his fragrant clasp of love,
When you go across the flooding streams
And the black river of death.

May Mary Virgin's Son himself
Be a generous lamp to you,
To guide you over
The great and awful ocean of eternity.

The compassing of the saints be upon you,
The compassing of the angels be upon you;
Of the compassing of all the saints
And of the nine angels be upon you.

May God's blessing be yours,
And well may it befall you.

The grace of the great God be upon you,
The grace of the Virgin Mary's Son be upon
    you,
The grace of the perfect Spirit be upon you,
Mildly and generously.

May God's goodness be yours,
And well and seven times well
May you spend your lives.

The love of your Creator be with you.

May Brigit and Mary and Michael
Shield you on sea and on land,
Each step and each path you travel.

Be the eye of God dwelling with you,
The foot of Christ in guidance with you,
The shower of the Spirit pouring on you,
Richly and generously.

God's peace be to you,
Jesus' peace be to you,
Spirit's peace be to you
And to your children,
Oh to you and to your children,
Each day and night
Of your portion in the world.

The love and affection of the angels be to you,
The love and affection of the saints be to you,
The love and affection of heaven be to you,
To guard you and to cherish you.

The compassing of the King of life be yours,
The compassing of loving Christ be yours,
The compassing of Holy Spirit be yours
Unto the crown of the life eternal,
Unto the crown of the life eternal.

My own blessing be with you,
The blessing of God be with you,
The blessing of Spirit be with you
And with your children,
With you and with your children.

The guarding of the God of life be on you,
The guarding of loving Christ be on you,
The guarding of Holy Spirit be on you
Every night of your lives,
To aid you and enfold you
Each day and night of your lives.

My own blessing be with you,
The blessing of God be with you,
The blessing of saints be with you
And the peace of the life eternal,
Unto the peace of the life eternal.

May God shield you on every steep,
May Christ aid you on every path,
May Spirit fill you on every slope,
On hill and on plain.

May the King shield you in the valleys,
May Christ aid you on the mountains,
May Spirit bathe you on the slopes,
In hollow, on hill, on plain,
Mountain, valley and plain.

The shape of Christ be towards me,
The shape of Christ be to me,
The shape of Christ be before me,
The shape of Christ be behind me,
The shape of Christ be over me,
The shape of Christ be under me,
The shape of Christ be with me,
The shape of Christ be around me
On Monday and on Sunday;
The shape of Christ be around me
On Monday and on Sunday.

The love and affection of heaven be to you,
The love and affection of the saints be to you,
The love and affection of the angels be to you,
The love and affection of the sun be to you,
The love and affection of the moon be to you,
Each day of your lives,
To keep you from haters, to keep you from
    harmers,
To keep you from oppressors.

The peace of God be with you,
The peace of Christ be with you,
The peace of Spirit be with you
And with your children,
From the day that we have here today,
To the day of the end of your lives,
Until the day of the end of your lives.

The grace of God be with you,
The grace of Christ be with you,
The grace of Spirit be with you
And with your children,
For an hour, for ever, for eternity.

God's grace distil on you,
Christ's grace distil on you,
Spirit's grace distil on you
Each day and each night
Of your portion in the world;
Oh each day and each night of your portion in
   the world.

God's blessing be yours,
And well may it befall you;
Christ's blessing be yours,
And well may you be entreated;
Spirit's blessing be yours,
And well spend you your lives,
Each day that you rise up,
Each night that you lie down.

May the eye of the great God,
The eye of the God of glory,
The eye of the Virgin's Son,
The eye of the gentle Spirit
Aid you and shepherd you
In every time,
Pour upon you every hour
Mildly and generously.

Holy Christ, bless me with Thy presence
when my days are weary and my friends few.
Bless me with Thy presence when my joy is
   full,
lest I forget the Giver in the gift.
Bless me with thy presence when I shall make
   an end of living.

Help me in the darkness to find the ford.
And in my going comfort me with thy promise
that where thou art, there shall thy servant
  be.

Hebridean Blessing[17]

A Hymn of Praise

Blessing and brightness,
wisdom, thanksgiving,
great power and might
to the King who rules over all.

Glory and honour and goodwill,
praise and sublime song of minstrels,
exceeding love from every heart
to the King of heaven and earth.

To the chosen Trinity has been joined
before all, after all, universal
blessing and everlasting blessing,
blessing and everlasting blessing.

Ninth century, Old Irish (translated by Oliver Davies)

References

1   *Rite for the Blessing of Water.* English translation of the *Roman Missal*, International Committee on English in the Liturgy, Inc. (ICEL) 1983.
2   (and see Reference 15 below) *Carmina Gadelica*, a collection of poems and songs by Alexander Carmichael, Scottish Academic, Edinburgh, 1976.
3   For inspiration in writing this blessing, I owe thanks to *The Appendix of Blessings, National Liturgical Commission 1977.*
4   *The Appendix of Blessings.*
5   *The Appendix of Blessings.*
6   From Brendan O'Malley, *A Pilgrim's Manual, St David's*, Paulinus Press, 1985.
7   A. Llwyd, A Rhydwen Williams in *Gwynn ap Gwilym*, Gomer/Barddas, 1986.
8   *The Appendix of Blessings.*
9   The Northumbria Community, *Celtic Daily Prayer*, Harper Collins, 1994.
10 David Adam, *The Edge of Glory, prayers in the Celtic tradition*, Triangle, 1985.
11 St Hilda Community, *Women Included*, SPCK, 1991.
12 This and the following four blessings are from *Women Included.*
13 David Adam, *The Edge of Glory.*
14 This and the following four blessings are from David Adam, *The Open Gate*, Triangle, 1994.
15 All the prayers on this page are from David Adam, *The Open Gate.*
16 This and the following thirty-two blessings are from *Carmina Gadelica.*
17 Alastair Mclean, *Hebridean Altars*, The Moray Press, 1937.

Further books from The Canterbury Press catalogue

PILGRIM GUIDES

Each year, our great cathedrals, abbeys and other holy places attract millions of visitors—and each year the numbers rise. These illustrated, reflective guides look beyond the historical and architectural riches and enable visitors and pilgrims alike to connect with the hidden spiritual dimension which makes these pilgrim places so powerfully inviting.

64pp   167x113mm   paperback   illustrated   £3.99 each

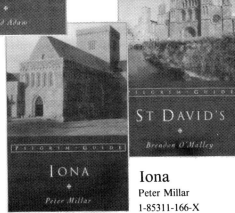

Holy Island
David Adam
1-85311-165-1

St David's
Brendan O'Malley
1-85311-168-6

Iona
Peter Millar
1-85311-166-X

Also available in the series: Canterbury, Durham, Salisbury, Winchester and York. Ely, North Yorkshire and St Albans to follow in April 1998, Norwich, Tewkesbury and Aylesford in July 1998.

God at Every Gate – prayers and blessings for pilgrims

Brendan O'Malley

This is a prayer book for every pilgrim, whether undertaking a real journey or regarding each day as part of our pilgrimage towards God. For every stage along the journey, for every need felt – physical, emotional or spiritual, for all seasons and all weathers, this anthology provides short outlines for thanksgiving, reflection and prayer. Equally good for globetrotters and armchair travellers alike!

1-85311-162-7   192pp   180x105mm   paperback   illustrated   £5.99

Celtic Gifts – orders of ministry in the Celtic church

Robert van de Weyer

Before the Roman pattern of church government was introduced, a vigorous and strong Celtic church was thriving and growing in the British Isles with its own orders of ministry and service. Teachers and healers, missionaries and hermits, monks, bishops and priests had a distinctively Celtic understanding of their calling. This original book sheds new light on the way we regard various forms of ministry.

1-85311-158-9   96pp   198x126mm   paperback   £5.99